Murder on the Largo

Henry Coleman and New Mexico's Last Frontier

Eleanor Williams
Edited with an Introduction by Jerry Thompson

Number 23 in the A. C. Greene Series

University of North Texas Press
Denton, Texas

10 9 8 7 6 5 4 3 2 1

Permissions:
University of North Texas Press
1155 Union Circle #311336
Denton, TX 76203-5017

The paper used in this book meets the minimum requirements of the American
National Standard for Permanence of Paper for Printed Library Materials,
z39.48.1984. Binding materials have been chosen for durability.

Library of Congress Cataloging-in-Publication Data

Names: Williams, Eleanor, 1906–1979, author.
Title: Murder on the Largo : Henry Coleman and New Mexico's last frontier /
   Eleanor Williams.
Other titles: Henry Coleman and New Mexico's last frontier
Description: Denton, Texas : University of North Texas Press, [2024] |
   Series: A.C. Greene series ; number 23 | Original title "Outlaw Born Too
   Late," published under the pseudonym Mel Jewell, was printed in eight
   installments from August 1964 to March 1965 in "New Mexico Electric
   News." | Includes bibliographical references and index.
Identifiers: LCCN 2024033890 (print) | LCCN 2024033891 (ebook) |
ISBN 9781574419337 (cloth) | ISBN 9781574419429 (ebook)
Subjects: LCSH: Coleman, Henry, 1871?-1921. | Outlaws--New
   Mexico--Biography. | Ranch life--New Mexico. | Murder--New
   Mexico--History--19th century. | Murder--New Mexico--History--20th
   century. | New Mexico--History--1848- | New Mexico--Biography. | BISAC:
   HISTORY / United States / State & Local / Southwest (AZ, NM, OK, TX) |
   BIOGRAPHY & AUTOBIOGRAPHY / Criminals & Outlaws
Classification: LCC F801.C75 W55 2024 (print) | LCC F801.C75 (ebook) |
   DDC 978.905092 [B]--dc23/eng/20240822
LC record available at https://lccn.loc.gov/2024033890
LC ebook record available at https://lccn.loc.gov/2024033891

Murder on the Largo is Number 23 in the A. C. Greene Series.

Publication of this book was supported by a grant from the Provost and the Dean of the
College of Arts and Sciences, Texas A&M International University.

The electronic edition of this book was made possible by the support of the Vick
Family Foundation. Typeset by vPrompt eServices.

Henry Coleman was one of the very last
of the bad men of New Mexico.

—Elfego Baca, sheriff, Socorro County

Contents

Introduction by Jerry Thompson   1

Murder on the Largo by Eleanor Williams   21

Chapter 1   A Place Called Quemado   23

Chapter 2   South of the Border   31

Chapter 3   Homesteading   39

Chapter 4   Shenanigans   45

Chapter 5   On the Zuni Trail   49

Chapter 6   Outlaw Born too Late   57

Chapter 7   Clara Coleman   69

Chapter 8   Trust in a Lawless Land   77

Chapter 9   Murders on the Largo   85

Photo Gallery

Chapter 10   Self-Defense   109

Chapter 11   More Shenanigans   115

Chapter 12   A Trial and a Marriage   123

Chapter 13   Indictments without End   135

Chapter 14   Death at the Goat Ranch   143

Epilogue   159

Life of Eleanor Williams
by Helen Cress 167

Bibliography 175

Index 183

Introduction

Jerry Thompson

C oming of age in the mountains of western New Mexico in the early 1950s, I distinctly remember setting around a campfire late one evening with my father and grandfather and hearing the remarkable story of Henry Coleman. Especially spellbinding were the recollections of how Coleman was involved in several grisly murders. Also intriguing was how he died so violently at the hands of a sheriff's posse in October 1921 at a place called the Goat Ranch, thirty remote miles northwest of the small village of Quemado, in the vast and rugged canyon lands of New Mexico near the Arizona border.

There were rugged and tough men still living in those days who had known Coleman personally and who could not resist relating tales of his audacious deeds. Emotions were still raw in Catron County at the time, and there were frequent debates as to Coleman's guilt or innocence. Those who had known Coleman seemed to either admire him as a man of honor and great courage or despise him as a worthless and deceitful rustler and murderer. No one seemed indifferent. Coleman had become to Catron County what Billy the Kid was to Lincoln County: a larger-than-life character whose legacy seemed

only to grow with the passing of time. My father often repeated many
of the tales, and I think he had a lifelong desire to acquire the pistol
Coleman had when he was gunned down at the Goat Ranch.

"One Mean Son of a Bitch"

Many people in western New Mexico were afraid of Coleman and
went out of their way to avoid him. Even the celebrated Socorro
County Sheriff, Elfego Baca, who crossed paths with Coleman several
times, was careful not to antagonize him. One time when Coleman
was arrested and waiting to post bond, Baca allowed him to stay in
a fashionable Socorro hotel rather than the county jail. There is little
doubt that Coleman could be dangerous. Kind and courteous to some,
he could be heartless and offensive to others. He would kill you with
little provocation, they said. The legendary rancher John Thomas
"Salty John" Cox, in an interview toward the end of his life in 1953,
remembered Coleman as "a good looking, well-dressed man, but one
mean son of a bitch." Cox concluded, "I'll tell you what kind of man
he was. He was the kind of man who would kill people, then go back
and rob their orphans."[1]

The charismatic Coleman was certainly someone you did not want
to offend. When he walked into a restaurant or tavern in Quemado,
Magdalena, or even Socorro, silence prevailed. Others, including
many of the Hispanics living on the large ranches and small farms
in the Quemado area, respected Coleman, rode with him, and had
fond, heartfelt memories of the man. Coleman was fluent in Spanish,
and they seemed to enjoy his company. D. B. Baca, who served as
justice of the peace in Quemado off and on for thirty years, knew
Coleman well and remembered how Henry would stand in front of his
mercantile store, "toss a tin can in the air, and put three bullets through
it before it hit the ground." Coleman would triumphantly "twirl his
six-shooter in his hands between each shot," Baca said.[2]

Roaming the untamed expanses of western New Mexico, Coleman
was a larger-than-life relic right out of the Old West, a cowboy who

carried a six-shooter low on his right hip and went everywhere on horseback. He was a Wild West character that outlived the Wild West, or as the noted artist and writer Eleanor Williams put it, an "outlaw born too late." He made the Wild West wild again. No one was more fascinated by the troubled legacy of Henry Coleman than Williams. She was certain Coleman's biography was worth telling, and she interviewed everyone she could find who had known him.

A trick rider with Ringling Brothers and Barnum and Bailey in her early life and an accomplished horsewoman, Williams had settled on a ranch on Largo Creek close to where it was said Coleman murdered several people. Williams proved to be an excellent sleuth as she wound her way through court records in Socorro and Reserve in an attempt to grab glimpses of Coleman's forceful and violent life. We are all fortunate for her energy and fortitude. Without her efforts, much of the history of Coleman and the early history of Catron County would be lost.

A Jail in Ciudad Juárez

Coleman had first come to the attention of the New Mexico and Texas press in 1895, when he was arrested in Ascensión, Mexico, along with John Ward and Israel King. Charged with cattle rustling from the Mormon colony in Chihuahua, he was sentenced to four years in prison. When bail was denied, two of Coleman's younger brothers, Claude and Roy Hudspeth, hastened west from their ranch headquarters at Juno on the Devils River and concocted the idea of throwing a rope over the prison wall in Ciudad Juárez where Coleman was being held and pulling their brother to safety. One of Coleman's cowboy friends, John Cox, tried the stunt and, when it failed, was barely able to escape a fusillade from Mexican guards.[3]

After a year in the Juárez prison, Coleman, largely with the help of his brothers, was able to bribe one of the guards. He and another American, Jim Dowell, made it over the wall with a third inmate in the early morning hours of November 20, 1896. Spotted by some

Mexican cavalrymen, the three escapees ran off in the darkness into the mountains west of Juárez and eventually waded across the Rio Grande to safety.[4] Henry and his brothers were said to have received several "warm congratulations."[5]

After Henry's narrow escape, he and his wife, Clara, settled down on a ranch in the desert foothills of the Little Florida Mountains, seven miles southeast of Deming, where he was able to claim almost two sections of land.[6] Eight years earlier the 1900 census indicated he was living with his 30-year-old wife, Clara, whom he had married, probably in Mexico, on Gold Avenue in downtown Deming. At the time Henry Coleman listed his occupation as "Cattle Raiser." In 1904 Coleman was in the forefront of a gold rush in the eastern foothills of the Black Range near Hillsboro. The placer mining on Palomas Creek never amounted to much, and he quickly returned to his ranch in the Little Floridas.[7] Dehorning as many as eight hundred stock at a time, Coleman was referred to by the local press as the "successful cattle man of the Floridas."[8] Although from Texas, he was described as "one of the old time cowboys of New Mexico" who had lived a "varied and somewhat thrilling experience during his residence in the Sunshine Territory."[9] Many of the hundreds of stock Coleman shipped from the stockyards in Deming, however, appear to have been stolen in Mexico. Regardless, by 1904 Coleman was so popular in Deming that the Luna County Democratic Party nominated him for sheriff. Four years later, however, he was charged with wire cutting and was hauled into federal court in Las Cruces. In a "hotly and stubbornly fought" case lasting ten days, Coleman and a codefendant, Albert Keith, were acquitted.[10]

Into the Badlands

From Deming Henry and Clara headed north to the vast windswept plains and towering mountains of western New Mexico, and it was here that Eleanor Williams picks up the trail. At the time, the western half of Socorro County was New Mexico's last frontier. The remote land had always been wild and colorful. Here were vast piñon and ponderosa pine forests as far as the eye can see, perhaps the largest in North America, as well as endless spans of black volcanic-topped mesas, grasslands that stretch to the horizon, and the sacred Zuni Salt Lake. Nestled against the Arizona border, halfway between Colorado and Mexico, the western half of Socorro County, which became Catron County in 1921, was for several decades a lawless, violent land—so much so that sheriffs in Socorro were reluctant to send their deputies riding west for three days.

Catron County remains the largest in the state with the fewest people per square mile, the southern half of the county encompassing the vast and grand Gila Wilderness, the first and the largest area designated "wilderness" in the United States. In the high county of western New Mexico, the mild summers were legendary, although winters were cold and the snow often lay on the land for weeks.

Those Who Came Before

Long before Henry and Clara Coleman rode into the wilds of Socorro County to seek a new beginning near Quemado, others walked and lived on the land. As early as the tenth and eleventh centuries, the Mimbres or Mogollon peoples from the vast Chihuahuan and Sonoran Deserts to the south settled along the rivers and rivulets in the area. At the same time, Ancestral Puebloans moved in from the windswept Zuni Plateau to the north. The Mimbres and Puebloans built small primitive structures using adobe and rocks, covered with logs and dirt roofs. To catch the morning sun, dwellings were constructed on the southeast slopes of low-lying hills along the numerous watersheds. Henry and Clara seemed fascinated with the early settlers, and they dug their ruins, collected their arrowheads, and prized their artifacts.

A severe drought from around 1275 to 1300 forced the Native Americans to abandon their homes and migrate east to the Rio Grande. Over time their villages became ruins; all that remains today are piles of adobe and rocks. Broken pieces of pottery, grinding stones, and colorful shards litter the landscape.

In the centuries that followed, the Mangas and Gallo Mountains became a boundary line between the Diné, who, along with their Zuni and Acoma neighbors, inhabited the vast plateaus and table-lands to the north, and the Chiricahua Apache, who roamed the rough, broken Mogollon Rim and the desert uplands to the south. Geronimo, or Goyaalé (He Who Yawns), of the Bedonkohe band of Apache, was born here on the headwaters of the Gila River in June 1829. The most significant Apache war chief of the nineteenth century, Mangas Coloradas, a tall and striking Mimbreño, was also born in the region sometime between 1790 and 1795.

Slave Raiders and Men in Blue

Violent change came with Spanish exploration and colonization in the fifteenth and sixteenth centuries. Even after Mexican inde-pendence in 1821, Hispano slave-raiding expeditions from the Rio Grande Valley and Ute marauders from the north terrorized the Native American populations of the area. Later, during the American Civil War, violence against the Navajo (Diné) and the Apaches (Ndé) intensified. Army patrols from Fort Craig on the Rio Grande to the southeast, Fort Wingate near El Malpais to the northeast, and, for a short time, Fort West on the Gila River to the south repeatedly pene-trated the area, burning hogans, razing wickiups, killing livestock, and destroying what little agriculture that existed. During many of the forays, Hispano soldiers in the New Mexico Volunteers and Territorial Militia took a liking to the limitless grasslands, small creeks, and towering mountains in this vast land.[11]

One such soldier was Pvt. José María Madrid, who served in the First New Mexico Cavalry during the Civil War and was on several expeditions into the area. About 1873, in the midst of an Apache war, Madrid established a small sheep ranch at Rito Quemado, near a clear water creek northeast of Escondido Mountain. Rito Quemado took its name from either the Navajos or the Apaches having burned the sage and rabbit brush along the creek or, as some say, a Native American leader by that name from the area. It is uncertain whether Largo Creek to the west, which twisted north out of the Gallo Mountains, took its name from José Largo, a prominent Diné chieftain who lived in the area, or the fact the creek was one of the longer, more prominent ones in the area. These Navajo appear to have been quite distinctive from the larger Navajo tribe around Canyon de Chelly and in the Four Corners area.

Hispanos in a Violent Land

Madrid's brother-in-law, José Antonio Padilla, who also served in the military during the Civil War, fought rebel Texans, and escorted Navajos to the Bosque Redondo, arrived with a large herd of sheep from Belen. Padilla did much to start the livestock industry in the area. In its early years, the *Albuquerque Journal* complained that Rito Quemado had become the "rendezvous for a bad gang of outlaws."[12]

Across the mountains to the south, Fort Tularosa was established at the head of the Tularosa Valley in 1872 to guard a short-lived Apache reservation along the river for as many as 450 people of the Warm Springs, Coyotero, and Mimbreño tribal subgroups. The Apaches, who had never wanted to leave the much warmer area along the upper Cañada Alamosa at Ojo Caliente, thought the winters in the high country too cold. They returned south after only two years, and the post was deactivated.[13]

West-central New Mexico was the last area of the state to be occupied by outside settlers. So remote was the small village of Rito Quemado that for years authorities in Santa Fe, with no accurate map of the area, thought the small community was in Valencia County. About this time, twelve miles southeast, at the foot of Mangas Mountain, three small villages were established by seven families in the more verdant Mangas Valley, which quickly became the headquarters for several large sheep ranches. By 1883 twelve families were living at Rito Quemado and fourteen in the Mangas Valley. Other Hispanos settled along the San Francisco River Valley to the southwest.

By the mid-1880s, in the Gallo Mountains southwest of Rito Quemado, gunmen of the American Valley Cattle and Sheep Company, many of them transplanted Texans, reigned supreme. From their headquarters on the headwaters of Largo Creek, the company came to control vast grasslands and pastures where as many as twelve thousand head of sheep and thousands of cattle grazed. The man who came to be the center of the ranching empire was Missouri-born Thomas Benton Catron, a University of Missouri alumnus who had served as a Confederate artillery officer during the Civil War. Catron had come to New Mexico after the war, learned Spanish, studied law, and became part of a group of notorious land speculators called the Santa Fe Ring. Catron was able to gain an interest or clear title to thirty-four Spanish land grants totaling more than three million acres and quickly became the largest landowner in the territory, surpassing Lucien Maxwell and the Maxwell Land Grant. Catron was also a principal investor in the American Valley Company.

Catron and others in the sheep and cattle industry hoped to expand their vast holdings by having the company's cowboys file endless homestead claims. The land fraud corruption that existed in Santa Fe, especially in the office of Henry Atkinson, the surveyor general, was also an asset for Catron and other members of the Santa Fe Ring who controlled the company.[14]

Cattle, Sheep, and Gunmen

Principal victims of the gunmen of American Valley were the Hispanics at Rito Quemado and in the Mangas Valley. Numerous Hispanos, not aware of the land laws in the territory, were either driven off their land by legal shenanigans and corrupt lawyers or through intimidation and violence. In some instances the Hispanos fought back.[15]

In December 1882 cattlemen, largely led by American Valley, assembled at Socorro to create the Cattlemen's Protective Association. The cattlemen hoped to head off the Gila Monsters, a band of rustlers who were lurking in the Datil Mountains, and a second band to the

west operating along Apache Creek, or Rustler's Roost, as it was sometimes known. These rustlers would steal cattle and then drive the stock
to Socorro and even Albuquerque and Santa Fe. Daniel H. McAllister,
manager of American Valley and a deacon in the Mormon church,
was appointed to head a group of deputies to apprehend the thieves.
The leader of the Gila Monsters had been pursued by Hispanos to the
Arizona border and killed, but the rustlers proved resilient.[16]

By the 1880s Texas cowboys were flooding into the area; tensions
with Hispanic villagers along the Tularosa River reached a breaking
point. Many of the Texans arrived with prejudices against Hispanics
dating back to the Texas Revolution, the fall of the Alamo, and the Goliad
Massacre in 1836. Many of the Texans had a hard time adjusting to life in
a place where Hispanos dominated politics and much of the commerce.
Texas cattleman also resented the vast herds of Hispanic-owned sheep
that competed with their cattle for water and grazing lands. The Texan's
arrogance and assertiveness seemed to know no bounds.

In an era before wells, windmills and manmade earthen ponds
became common. Whoever controlled the water controlled the land,
and the American Valley Company was determined to control as much
of the water as possible. As the saying goes, "Whiskey is for drinking;
water is for fighting over."[17]

Murder at Gallo Springs

In the spring of 1880, before Catron bought into the American Valley
Company, the moving force behind the company, John P. Casey, drove
cattle into the area from Texas and established the ranch headquarters
on Largo Creek. Within a few years, partly through fraudulent land
claims, he managed to control some twelve thousand acres of patented
land and claim the water and grazing rights on as much as two to three
million acres across several townships. Hoping to sell out to wealthy
investors in the east and make a large profit, Casey anticipated pushing
the ranch holdings across Jewett Gap into the Gallo Basin on the south
side of the Gallo Mountains.

In the basin two homesteaders, Alexis Grossetete and Robert Elsinger, built a small log cabin near Gallo Springs and were holding on to the water. Casey tried repeatedly to purchase the homestead holdings from Grossetete and Elsinger. When they refused to sell, he turned to threats and intimidation. He finally brought in several hired guns and resorted to violence. On May 6, 1883, Casey's brother, James, and four hired gunmen from American Valley—Mueller Scott, W. C. Moore, James McIntyre, and James Courtright—murdered Grossetete and Elsinger in the woods south of the Gallo Mountains.[18]

Early that Sunday morning, Grossetete and Elsinger had hitched two black mares to a small wagon and gone southwest along a rough mountain trail down Gallo Canyon to the ranch of Manuel Romero, where they borrowed a plow.[19] On the homesteaders' return to Gallo Springs, Casey and the gunmen intercepted them. The gunmen told Grossetete and Elsinger there was a warrant for their arrest, and they were disarmed and told to unhitch their wagon. Astride their unharnessed horses, continuing northeast along the rocky road, Grossetete and Elsinger were led off into the woods up a small trail and then murdered. Allegedly, Moore shouted out, "This is far enough," rode up behind Grossetete, pulled out his pistol, placed it behind the homesteader's left ear, and pulled the trigger. The bullet went through Grossetete's brain and came out his right eye. His lifeless body slid from his horse and he fell facedown in the dry earth. Elsinger jerked his horse away from the party and attempted to flee, but four rifle shots ripped into his body—three in the small of the back and one just below a shoulder blade. Almost motionless, his body seemed to balance on his horse before he too fell to the ground near a large ponderosa pine. Moore had given orders prior to the encounter that all members of the party were to shoot and thus be equally guilty of the crime, so he rode up and shot into Grossetete's body, the bullet passing into his body through his right arm.[20]

On the day of the murders, Clotilde Grossetete and her children heard a volley of shots to the south of the Grossetete cabin in the direction of Apache Mountain and feared the worst, especially when the two men did not return as expected. Monday morning they found the two black mares a short distance from the homestead, their harnesses still attached. After two sheepmen, Ramon Gonzales and Juan Peralta, found a corpse beside the trail down Gallo Canyon, Deputy Sheriff Patrick Higgins arrived with a small search party. Following the tracks of several horsemen, Peralta led the posse three miles southwest from Gallo Springs to where the body of Elsinger lay beside a big pine tree. It had been four days and the body was badly decomposed, the whiff of rotting flesh drifting through the forest. Grossetete's body was not found until Clotilde, who had gone along with the posse, detected a second scent, and the remains of her firstborn son were soon located. With tears rolling down her cheeks, she fell to her knees beside his corpse to weep and pray. Both bodies were wrapped in blankets and buried together in a single grave on a sunny slope, not far from the Grossetete cabin.[21]

Evading Justice

On the day of the murders, the gunmen had spurred their horses back across the Gallo Mountains to ranch headquarters on the Largo. They first schemed to blame the murders on Apaches or outlaws, but when this became implausible, they falsely arrested several innocent settlers and took them to Albuquerque for an appearance before the grand jury. When one of the American Valley gunmen, Daniel H. McAllister, came forth with what had really happened, the case quickly unraveled. Casey and Scott were indicted and arrested, but Moore, McIntyre, and Courtright fled the territory. After two Albuquerque trials in which jurors were bribed and perjury abounded, Casey and Scott were acquitted. W. C. Moore fled to Alaska, where he died in a drunken brawl. James Courtright returned to his native Texas, where he opened a private detective agency only to die in a Fort Worth gunfight with the notorious gambler Luke Short.[22]

A few years later, on June 10, 1890, a second Grossetete brother, 20-year-old Frederic Auguste, died in a gun battle at the head of Negrito

Creek in the Gila country. The violence involved two Texas brothers, Jarrette and John Davis, who were said to have made "derogatory remarks" about Fred's sister, Adella, at a dance in the village of Aragon. Grossetete worked for the large Y Ranch at the time and heard the Davis brothers, who worked for the V-Cross-T Ranch, were camped nearby. He headed for their camp to seek an apology. Finding the Davis brothers and other cowboys sitting around a campfire, Grossetete, although wearing a gun, demanded to fight with his fists. His demands were met by gunfire from the two brothers, one of the bullets striking Grossetete in the chest below his heart and spinning him around, but not before he got off several shots that killed the two brothers. Grossetete was bandaged, and a physician was summoned from the mining towns of Cooney or the larger nearby Mogollon. Fred Grossetete died in the night following a coughing spell. He was buried on the family's new homestead on Apache Creek. The Davis brothers were taken to the railhead town of Magdalena and then to Anson in Jones County, Texas, for burial.[23]

A year after the Gallo Springs murders, in February 1884, Deputy Sheriff Higgins was escorting an accused horse and cattle rustler, Hank Andrews, from Horse Springs to the jail in Socorro when a gang of masked men rode up with guns and hanged Andrews from the nearest tree. Several of the murderers were brought to trial, but none were convicted. There was other violence involving the American Valley.[24]

Epic Gunbattle at Middle Frisco

Tensions had reached a violent climax in the village of Middle Frisco in October 1884 when a 19-year-old deputy sheriff from Socorro named Elfego Baca arrested a cowboy named Charlie McCarthy for disorderly conduct. Besieged by at least twenty of John Bunyan Slaughter's rowdy and drunken cowboys, who were notorious for settling disputes with their fists and guns, Baca took refuge in Geronimo Armijo's small jacal in the village. In one of the more famous gun battles in the history of the American West, Baca survived for thirty-three hours, during which thousands of bullets were fired into the jacal. Over time Baca's courageous defense in Middle Frisco would come to be celebrated in the 1950s Walt Disney television series *Nine Lives of Elfego Baca.* Baca brought justice, at least for a few days, to a raw, restless, and remote part of New Mexico Territory.

Beginning in 1885 with the arrival of a branch line of the Atchison, Topeka, and Santa Fe Railway in Magdalena, thousands of sheep and cattle were being driven each year from as far away as St. Johns, Arizona, and the vast grasslands in the area to be shipped east. As many as 150,000 head of sheep and 21,600 of cattle were driven to Magdalena in 1919. More sheep, cattle, and wool were thought to have been shipped from Magdalena than any other place in the American West. In Magdalena liquor flowed freely and monte tables were common. In the town's many saloons, hard rock miners from nearby Kelly mingled and fought with thirsty cowboys and sheepherders who arrived after weeks on the trail. Magdalena was a wild town, and gun battles became a way of life.[25]

Carrejos and the Coopers

In western New Mexico, the introduction of barbed wire and the 1916 Stock Raising Homestead Act changed everything. Unlike Lincoln's 1862 Homestead Act, which promised 160 acres of "land for the landless," the new act gave settlers a full section of land, 640 acres, for ranching purposes. Ranchers who had grazed their herds on public lands for decades hated the arrival of "nesters," most of them Texans. By the early 1920s, the US land commissioner in Quemado, N. G. Baca, reported that homesteaders by the hundreds were arriving in the area and as many as ten land claims were being filed weekly.[26] The new homesteaders settled on land where water was not readily available, but wells could be dug by hand or by machine. In the end it was the windmill, not the Remington or Colt revolver, that won the Southwest.

In the vast expanses of the western part of the state, rustling became a way of life well into the twentieth century. By World War I, much of the rustling in the area was blamed on Clay C. Cooper, owner of the NH Ranch. The NH Ranch was less than two miles to the east of where Nellie Whiskers Carrejo had settled beneath the naked 8,123-foot summit of Queen's Head, a conspicuous promontory. Clay Cooper and his two sons, Bruce and Harmon, were repeatedly charged with rustling. It seemed they were selling excessive quantities of meat in Reserve, Magdalena, Socorro, and Springerville, Arizona. But they always maintained their innocence and managed to produce a fresh hide with their brand. They were frequently indicted, however, but Elfego Baca, already a legend in Socorro County, using every unorthodox maneuver in his wide repertoire of legal tricks, managed to save the Coopers from trial and possible prison.[27]

Gunfight at the NH Corral

In 1918, about the time Henry Coleman was gaining a reputation across Jewett Gap to the north for rustling cattle, matters came to a bloody climax at the NH Ranch. The Carrejos, Nellie and her sons, noticed some of their cattle were missing. The two families began to keep their distance; the Coopers were known to refer to the Carrejos as "half-breeds." When the Carrejos' Holstein milk cow came up missing, the Carrejos had had enough. Filing charges against the Coopers would probably result in an indictment, but it was almost certain that Elfego Baca, the Coopers' attorney, would obtain countless continuances as he had done in the past. Instead, the Carrejos—brothers Juan, Ambrosio, and Enrique—formed a small posse and decided to take the law into their own hands. Juan Carrejo enlisted the assistance of Candelario Chavez, a mounted policeman, along with Fidel Armijo, a sheep and cattle inspector, and a neighbor, Byrd Cochrain.[28]

Before dawn on May 11, 1918, the members of the Carrejo posse saddled their horses and rode for the NH Ranch. Nineteen-year-old

Enrique was sent to the Jewett Ranger Station not far from the Cooper ranch to prevent the Coopers from using the telephone to summon rustling friends from the Tularosa Valley or Reserve. As dawn broke over Slaughter Mesa to the east, the posse heard a rifle shot at the ranch corral and knew the Coopers were preparing to butcher Nellie Carrejo's cow. His fiery temper ablaze, Juan Carrejo was in the lead as the posse approached the ranch. Seeing the riders and realizing that trouble was possible, Clay Cooper tried to stall the posse with an offer of coffee. Carrejo defiantly reined his horse toward the corral, where Harmon and Bruce Cooper had just shot the Carrejo cow. Bruce Cooper grabbed his .30-30 rifle, shouting, "You dirty Mexican half-breeds, if you come in here, I'll kill you!" As Carrejo pulled his own .30-30 out of the scabbard, Bruce Cooper opened fire. The first shot missed, but the second tore into the front of Juan's saddle, only inches from his thigh. Ambrosio Carrejo, Fidel Armijo, and Bruce Cochrain dismounted and ran forth with rifles and pistols at the ready. "Bullets were flying in the gray dawn and echoing for miles around," Cochrain later recalled.[29]

In the ensuing gun battle, Juan Carrejo was seriously wounded, Clay and Bruce Cooper killed, and Harmon Cooper shot through his mustache, teeth, and mouth, the bullet lodging in the back of his neck. Both Harmon and Juan Carrejo were hurried off in separate cars, over the rocky road to Sand Flats, across the Continental Divide and the vast San Agustin Plains, and on to the hospital in Socorro. In the days that followed, Elfego Baca drove up in his fancy new touring car to attend the funeral of Bruce and Clay Cooper.[30]

After decades of isolation and settlers having to ride three or four days on horseback to reach the county seat in Socorro, Catron County was formed out of the western part of Socorro County in 1921, with Reserve (formerly Upper Frisco or Milligan's Plaza) as the county seat. In the original bill before the state legislature, the name of the county was intended to be Frisco, but at the last minute, some of Thomas Benton Catron's friends decided to change the name of the county to honor him; he died in May 1921 at the age of 80.

It was in this vast and untamed land that Coleman was able to claim a piece of property a few miles north of Quemado, where he quickly became a well-known visitor in the small community. It is here that Eleanor Williams, who had spent much of her life on a cattle ranch on the Largo and intimately knew the land and the people of the area, takes up the intriguing story of Henry Coleman. She begins by guiding the reader to a lonely spot a few miles west of Zuni Salt Lake, northwest of Quemado, to a place called the Goat Ranch.

What follows is Eleanor Williams's dramatic and captivating study of Henry Coleman's violent life and death. Williams published her study in eight parts in the relatively unknown *New Mexico Electric News* in 1964 and 1965. The monthly magazine was received by individuals in New Mexico who belonged to an electrical co-op, part of the Rural Electrification Authority (REA), one of Franklin D. Roosevelt's long-lasting New Deal programs. Some of the content has been rearranged and edited for clarity.

In October 2020 Claude Hudspeth, great-nephew of Henry Coleman, and his wife, Ginger, dedicated a large gravestone in the Magdalena Cemetery that replaced a barely readable, smaller marker, that read, "Henry Coleman, Died October 15, 1921." "He did kill some people," Claude told a staff writer for the Socorro *El Defensor Chieftain*, "but, at that time, it was still the wild west out here."[31]

Two years later in 2022, among Williams's many paintings, her daughter, Helen Cress, found seven black-and-white sketches the artist had drawn to illustrate her Coleman story that were never used by the *New Mexico Electric News*. All are incorporated in Williams's story that follows.

When Williams wrote her articles in the 1950s and 1960s, recollections of Coleman were still fresh and painful in the minds of many of the individuals Williams interviewed. For that reason many preferred to remain anonymous. As many of these persons as possible have been identified.

Notes

1. Howard Bryan's interview with Fred Landon in *True Tales of the American Southwest: Pioneer Recollections of Frontier Adventures* (Santa Fe: Clear Light, 1998), 57–68.

2. Bryan, *True Tales of the American Southwest*, 67–68.

3. *Albuquerque Democrat*, June 4, 1896; Hillsboro *Sierra County Advocate*, November 27, 1896, from the *El Paso Herald*, n.d.; *Deming Headlight*, November 27, 1896; Silver City *Eagle*, October 28 and December 2, 1896; and *San Angelo* (TX) *Standard*, October 24, 1896.

4. *Albuquerque Democrat*, June 4, 1896.

5. *Deming Headlight*, November 27, 1896.

6. *Deming Graphic*, July 10, 1908.

7. *Deming Graphic*, December 16, 1904. Also, Maureen G. Johnson, *Placer Gold Deposits of New Mexico* (Washington, DC; United States Government Printing Office, 1972), 25–26.

8. 12th Census (1900), Luna County, NM; *Deming Headlight*, May 18, 19; *Deming Graphic*, December 28, 1906, July 10, 1908, and January 11, 1909; *Santa Fe New Mexican*, May 30, 1907.

9. *Deming Graphic*, June 14, 1907.

10. *Deming Graphic*, October 23, 1908.

11. For military forays into the area, see *Santa Fe Gazette*, August 29, 1863, and March 19, 1864; and Jerry Thompson, *A Civil War History of the New Mexico Volunteers and Militia* (Albuquerque: University of New Mexico Press, 2015), 296–97.

12. *Las Vegas* (NM) *Gazette*, February 2, 1883, and March 3, 1883, quoting the *Albuquerque Journal*, n.d. For alleged political corruption in the precinct of Rito Quemado and Mangas that was thought to be in Valencia County, see *Las Vegas* (NM) *Daily Gazette*, November 7 and 22, 1882.

13. David Kayser, "The Southern Apache Agency," *El Palacio* 79, no. 2 (September 1973): 16–23; David Kayser, "Fort Tularosa: 1872–1874," *El Palacio* 79, no. 2 (September 1973): 24–29. Also see Dan L. Thrapp, *Victorio and the Mimbres Apaches* (Norman: University of Oklahoma Press, 1974), 131–75, 276–78.

14. David L. Caffey, *Chasing the Santa Fe Ring: Power and Privilege in Territorial New Mexico* (Albuquerque: University of New Mexico Press, 2014), 120–21.

15. *Albuquerque Republican*, n.d., reported in the *Weekly Phoenix Herald*, March 29, 1883.

16. *Lincoln County Leader* (Toledo, OR), December 9, 1882.

17. "Whiskey Is for Drinking; Water Is for Fighting Over," *Quote Investigator*, accessed August 19, 2024, https://quoteinvestigator. com/2013/06/03/whiskey-water/#.

18. For the best account of the American Valley murders, see Victor Westphall, "The American Valley Murders," *Ayer Hoy en Taos: Yesterday and Today in Taos County and Northern New Mexico* (Fall 1989), 3–9. See also Don Bullis, *Unsolved: New Mexico's American Valley Ranch Murders and other Mysteries* (Los Ranchos, NM: Rio Grande Books, 2013). Alexis Grossetete had married Clemence Porovde (orPouarde), daughter of a French-Canadian pioneer, in Socorro only nine days before his death. McIntyre also appears in the historical record as McIntire.

    The violence in western New Mexico was matched by even more violence, murder, and mayhem in eastern Arizona in the late 1880s when eighteen men were killed. See Edwardo O. Pagan, *Valley of the Guns: The Pleasant Valley War and the Trauma of Violence* (Norman: University of Oklahoma Press, 2018).

19. Romero patented 320 acres just east of Queen's Head Mountain in 1891, where a second bloody gunbattle would erupt in 1916 at the NH Ranch. See State Volume Patent for Manuel Romero, June 8, 1891, US Department of the Interior Bureau of Land Management, General Office Records, accessed July 5, 2022, https://glorecords. blm.gov/details/patent/default.aspx?accession=NM0110__.494&doc Class=STA&sid=pviome1i.pkv.

20. Westphall, "American Valley Murders," 5–6.

21. Westphall, "American Valley Murders," 6–7. Clotilde Grossetete's diary for 1893–95 is accessible at the Center for Southwestern Research at the University of New Mexico. For a history of the Grossetete family in New Mexico, see "All Results for Grossetete," Ancestry.com, https://www. ancestry.com/search/?name=_grossetete&event=_New+Mexico-USA.

22. Westphall, "American Valley Murders," 7–8.

23. The twin Davis brothers' slender marble headstones at Mount Hope Cemetery at Anson in East Texas state the two were "Murdered in New Mexico." Davis family legend holds that Fred Grossetete had worked as a cook for Jarrette Davis, who was the ranch foreman and had been stealing food and other supplies to support his family when he was dismissed and ordered off the ranch. Grossetete appeared at a roundup

and killed Jarrette Davis and then his younger brother, John, who was said to have survived for eighteen hours, dying early on the morning of June 11, 1890. *Fort Worth Star-Telegram*, February 21, 1954. For a firsthand account and more objective version of the gunbattle, see William French, *Some Recollections of a Western Ranchman, New Mexico, 1883–1899* (New York: Frederick A. Stokes, 1928), 191–92. A detailed account of the tragedy can be found in Bryan's *True Tales of the American Southwest* and in Bryan's articles in the *Albuquerque Tribune*, February 9, 12, 16, and 23, 1959. See also *Albuquerque Journal*, April 10 and 11, 1977. Some referred to Apache Creek at this time as Rustler's Roost.

24. Bryan, *True Tales of the American Southwest*, 122. Thomas Catron still owned remnants of the company when he died in 1921.

25. There have been several fragmented and incomplete histories of Magdalena. David Wallace Adams's highly engaging *Three Roads to Magdalena: Coming of Age in a Southwest Borderlands, 1890–1990* (Lawrence: University Press of Kansas, 2016) is an exception. In clear prose Adams relates the dramatic story of how Alamo Diné, Hispanics, and Anglos negotiated the social and cultural dynamics of the small livestock and mining community.

26. *Albuquerque Morning Journal*, August 13, 1920.

27. Jerry Thompson, "Gunfight at the NH Corral," *Wild West* 10 (April 1998), 42–47, 78.

28. Thompson, "Gunfight at the NH Corral."

29. Valerie Owen, *Byrd Cochrain of Dead Man's Corner* (Snyder, TX: Feather Press, 1972), 188.

30. Owen, *Byrd Cochrain*, 193.

31. John Larson, "Cattle Rustler's Grave Gets New Headstone," Socorro *El Defensor Chieftain*, October 8, 2020.

Murder on the Largo

Eleanor Williams

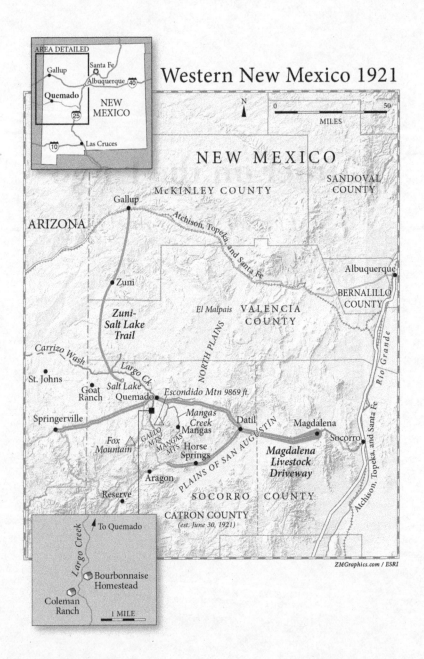

Western New Mexico 1921

AREA DETAILED

Gallup · Santa Fe
Albuquerque [40]
Quemado
NEW
MEXICO
[25]
Las Cruces
[10]

N

0   50
MILES

NEW MEXICO

McKINLEY COUNTY

SANDOVAL
COUNTY

ARIZONA

Gallup

Atchison, Topeka, and Santa Fe

Albuquerque

Zuni

BERNALILLO
COUNTY

*Zuni-
Salt Lake
Trail*

El Malpais

VALENCIA
COUNTY

NORTH PLAINS

Carrizo Wash

Largo Ck.

St. Johns

Salt Lake

Escondido Mtn 9869 ft.

Goat
Ranch

Quemado

Rio Grande

Springerville

*Mangas
Creek*
Mangas

Datil

Magdalena

Socorro

*Fox
Mountain*

GALLO MTN

MANGAS MTS

Horse
Springs

*Magdalena
Livestock
Driveway*

PLAINS OF SAN AUGUSTIN

Atchison, Topeka, and Santa Fe

Aragon

Reserve

SOCORRO   COUNTY

CATRON COUNTY
(est. June 30, 1921)

To Quemado

Largo Creek

Bourbonnaise
Homestead

Coleman
Ranch

1 MILE

ZMGraphics.com / ESRI

Chapter 1

A Place Called Quemado

Here is a true story of New Mexico, back in the days when there were more cattle, more rain, fewer fences, and more rustling. At least, the stealing was of a different nature from what it is today. It involved more skill and more hard work on the part of the individual because when cattle were stolen, they were usually driven on horseback for long distances—no loading into vans or trailers, or butchering on the spot. The man or men doing the stealing either drove the cattle off in bunches and took them a long way, or an individual with a long rope and the necessary skill would rope an animal, make a little fire, and run a brand on the animal right then and there. Nor was this stealing limited to the pros; most old-timers will give you a wry little smile and say, gently, "Most everybody stole; we had to steal to keep even."

Catron County, New Mexico, in those days was still part of huge sprawling Socorro County, and for the most part, unfenced. About the only fences then were little horse pastures; the range rolled away in grass-rich splendor for uninhibited, fence-free miles—hundreds of them. Waterings were mainly natural lakes and springs. Wells in those days were usually for house use and were largely hand-dug, not drilled. Nature's bounty in water seemed an eternal affair. The increasing cycles of drought had not yet posed any serious threat; the springs had not yet started to disappear and the lakes to go dry, although the country did have occasional droughts. Men who remember those days of the generous heavens above and the stirrup-high grass below shake their heads and hint that encroaching civilization was somehow responsible for the gradual and relentless shutdown of the heavenly faucets.

According to scholars, much of the erosion of the present time was caused by misuse of the land, particularly by overstocking. Old trails used by far too many cattle, they say, have bitten down into the earth and have caused the eroded gullies and arroyos. The genuine old-timers, almost to a man, insist that in the days of the open range there was no serious erosion problem, that there were many more cattle on the range—not only cattle but bands of wild horses and wild burros in countless numbers—and that there was plenty of grass for all.

Back in these days, at the turn of the century, a man known as Henry Coleman drifted into what is now Catron County and considerably stepped up the tempo of life in these parts. When I say that this is a true story, I must make some reservations and add that, as accurately as I was able to gather the facts, this story is true. But with a man of Henry's caliber and exploits, some amount of legend is bound to creep in and join hand in hand with the true and known facts. So, in the interests of honest reporting, I will give you both fact and legend, as they have been told to me. In some instances two or three different men who knew Henry would tell me the same story, but the versions would differ in some of the smaller details. I will present all the versions. Most of them are interesting, and altogether they add up to a colorful and authentic picture of a man who died as recently as 1921, yet who lived in the manner of some of the outlaws of the 1870s. He chose to live close to the land and he did a good job of it, with all the innovations of civilization already in full swing only a matter of a few hundred miles away. Sound movies themselves were only a few years away when Henry died, and Hollywood had already embarked upon its fantastic modus vivendi and was making Western films of bygone days, while Henry in the flesh, and with a certain innocence of his role, competed with them in authentic outlawry.

He was born Henry Hudspeth, a member of an old, respected family in southwestern Texas. Hudspeth County in West Texas was named after Henry's brother, Claude Hudspeth, a well-known lawyer and legislator, known in the latter part of his life as Senator Hudspeth. Henry himself had talents for legal maneuvering, had he chosen to be a lawyer. While he was living in the Quemado area, he once defended a friend who had found himself in a scrape of some sort, and Henry took the part of the defense with no little skill.[1] In those days anyone who had a few law books, an agile mind, and an articulate tongue could go into court and act as a lawyer, without the formality of a law degree or a license to practice law. It was said that Henry at some time in his life studied law, perhaps from books he received from his brother.

In the absence of actual photographs of Henry, I drew descriptions from different men who knew him. Said one, "Henry was a dark-complexioned slender man with hazel eyes that could look clear through you. And very alert; no one ever slipped up on him." Another said of him, "Henry—you couldn't enjoy being with him. He was like a caged lion, so restless that he could never relax. He could smile at you and then kill you; you never knew what he was thinking about or what he was getting ready to do."

One woman described his eyes as blue. "He had steel-blue eyes that could look right through you," she said. People might not have always remembered accurately, but something about his eyes seemed to stay with them all. Another man said, "He had the strangest eyes of any man I ever saw, alert and penetrating. I only saw one other man in my life that had eyes like that, and he was a killer too."

In talking to one old-timer, I was impressed by the impact of a singular superior memory and by the sincerity of the man himself. He looked directly at me as he spoke, and his way of telling a story showed that he was one of those very observing individuals, the kind who sees the little things as well as the larger ones, who could go

back into the past and draw out memories that have been neatly and accurately stored away. "I never forget a person's eyes," he said. "Henry's eyes were a dark hazel color and had little specks in them." He went on to tell me that Henry was a man of average height, probably about five feet eight or nine, with wide shoulders but slender otherwise. He verified what others had said, that Henry always wore a small Stetson hat with no crease in the crown. He usually wore a Colt .45 repeater on his right hip, low down. Henry had dark curly hair, he said, and a ruddy complexion and was very clean-cut. This man also gave another detail, which showed his powers of observation plus his good memory, because no one else seems to have remembered this about Henry: "He always wore his hair combed down over his forehead," he said. "That was to hide an old scar where a bullet had once grazed his forehead."

Everyone agreed that Henry had impeccable manners, if one met him in a casual way. He was quiet-spoken, dressed very neatly, and gave the impression of having been well educated. He always rode good horses and had a reputation for being a dead shot with a pistol, as well as for being as quick a draw as all the traditional gunmen of the 1800s. He could occasionally advertise his marksmanship by casually stopping a bird in flight with one quick, sure shot, or he could throw a tin can into the air and drill a hole through it before it fell to earth. Either he was advertising or practicing! But the exhibitions he gave were consistently sensational, and this seems to have been more on the side of fact than of fiction, as there are too many tales of his prowess with a gun for them all to be legendary.

Coleman did not attempt to obscure his early life from those who came to know him in Catron County. All that I could learn of his previous life came from a man who knew his family in Texas and had heard the story of one of his scrapes. A marriage certificate issued to Henry in Socorro County in 1920 shows his date of birth as February 20, 1871, in San Angelo, Texas.[2]

For a man of Henry's intelligence, his outlawry presents us with an enigma. What caused him, a man of whom it was said on every hand, "He was smart; he had the nicest manners you ever say; he had a good education," to turn outlaw? That takes us back to the late 1890s, when outlaws were spawned with frequency. At this time Henry was working on a roundup at a place called Pan Flats, about twenty miles out of San Angelo. One big outfit had a large herd of cattle rounded up, and Henry and some others were there representing their own interests or those of some other ranch—"repping," as it was known in those days. Evidently, from what followed, Henry had already become quite proficient with a six-shooter. Perhaps the boss of the outfit was unaware. Anyway, the manager told Henry that he could ride down one side of the herd to look at the brands. But, he specified, Henry was not to come over on the other side, where the boss and his men were. What started the shooting is unclear, but Henry and several others refused to comply with the boss's orders. When the gun smoke cleared away, several men lay dead or wounded. Henry had a scar near his chin when he came to Quemado, and the one he combed his hair over, but whether these were made at that particular encounter is uncertain. The man who told me the story of this gun battle was of the opinion that Henry and maybe several other survivors had to leave the area and wound up in Mexico, which was not far away.

Notes

1. Since the inception of this project to publish Eleanor Williams's manuscript, Claude Hudspeth, great-nephew of Henry Coleman, has taken an active interest. Claude assisted in archival sleuthing and dedicated a grave marker to Coleman at the Magdalena (NM) Cemetery. Several times at a moments' notice, Hudspeth drove from his home near San Angelo, Texas, to view the remains of Clara Coleman's homestead, her gravesite in Quemado, or what remains of the remote Goat Ranch and the hillside where Coleman died.

2. In 1880 the Hudspeth family was living on the Medina River at Bandera in Bandera County, Texas, twenty-five miles northwest of San Antonio. The family patriarch, Mississippi-born Henry Street Hudspeth Jr., was a retired schoolteacher. The son, Henry Street Hudspeth, who later changed his name to Coleman, was eight at the time and named after his father. He was one of six children, and the second oldest son in the family. In June 1861, at the beginning of the Civil War, Henry Coleman's father enlisted in Company C, the Confederate Stars of the 3rd Arkansas Infantry at Monticello, and rose through the ranks to become a captain. The regiment was the most celebrated from Arkansas. It was also the only Arkansas regiment to serve throughout the war in the Army of Northern Virginia in the eastern theatre. Of the 134 men who enlisted in Company C at Monticello, only 13 were at Appomattox Court House in April 1865.

     The family had migrated to Texas in 1877 from Marion in Drew County, Arkansas, not far from Monticello. This was in the poverty-ridden south-central part of the state, where an older brother, Landrus, younger brother, Claude, and an older sister, Mary, were born and where his father, Henry Street, taught school. Before and after their settlement in Bandera County, Texas, at least forty other members of the family, including the Bandera County treasurer, a physician, a lawyer, and at least two other individuals that were named Henry Street Hudspeth, all came to Texas. The census enumerator in 1880 noted that the younger Henry was "at school," while his father was "maimed or bed-ridden." Coleman's father eventually became sheriff of Bandera County. The family later moved to Ozona in Crockett County, where Henry's father became county clerk. When Henry's brother, state senator Claude Benton Hudspeth, first ran for congress in 1918, he frequently made reference to being a native Texan and having been "born in a little cabin on the banks of the Medina River." His political opponent, Zach Lamar Cobb, a carpetbagger from Georgia, pointed out that Hudspeth had really been born in Arkansas and that there were several people in Bandera who could affirm this. The 1880 census clearly enumerates Claude Hudspeth as having been born in Arkansas. Internet and printed references to Claude Benton Hudspeth, nevertheless, list his birth as May 12, 1877, in Medina, Texas, as he claimed. In 1910 Henry Coleman's younger sister, Mary Elizabeth, joined the faculty of what was then West Texas State Normal College (now West Texas A&M University), where she taught languages, literature, and Spanish and went on to become the college's first dean of women. In Canyon she acquired a spacious residence where she housed students. Georgia O'Keeffe, who was head of the art department at the university from 1916 to 1918, frequently took meals at the residence.

In Deming, New Mexico, in 1900, Henry Coleman told the census enumerator he was born in 1875. Ten years later he told the census enumerator in Luna County he was born "about 1873." In 1920, near Quemado in what was then Socorro County, he told the enumerator he was born "about 1871." Yet for the marriage certificate in Quemado in 1921, he told a justice of the peace he had been born in San Angelo, Texas, on February 20, 1871. From the 1880 census, it is evident that he and his siblings, except for his younger sister, Maggie, were all born in Arkansas. See: 9th Census (1870), Drew County, AR; 10th Census (1880), Bandera County, TX; 12th Census (1900), Crockett County, TX, and Luna County, NM; 13th Census (1910) and 14th Census (1920), Socorro County, NM, National Archives; "Hudspeth Native of Arkansas, Not Texas, Say Bandera People," *El Paso Herald*, July 13, 1918; Martin Donell Kohout, "Claude Benton Hudspeth (1877–1941)," *Handbook of Texas Online*, accessed May 27, 2021, https://www.tshaonline.org/handbook/entries/hudspeth-claude-benton; "Claude Benton Hudspeth (1877–1941)," *Biographical Dictionary of the United States Congress, 1774–Present*, accessed May 27, 2021, https://bioguideretro.congress.gov/Home/MemberDetails?memIndex=H000910.

Chapter 2

South of the Border

For several years Henry worked in Mexico, where he represented and even ran several big American cattle outfits. In those days any of the best American cowboys were south of the border, and for many different reasons.[1] Henry could speak Spanish like a native. The very nature of the wild country and the way of life there allowed for no weaklings. His comings and goings in Mexico were never accounted for with any degree of accuracy—which, after all, is what he went there for! For years he would drift back to the United States and then back to Mexico again—in and out. He knew his way around the border, and he rounded out his education—his way of living—in a country teeming with other outlaws and revolutionaries, and with an almost total absence of greenhorns or amateurs. If there were any of the latter, they never lasted long enough to go on record.

If we could paint a picture of life in Old Mexico at that time, we would probably come up with a pretty colorful canvas. There were some reputable cow outfits run like any others, but with more freedom. There was plenty of room for shady characters, men using assumed names and on the dodge, men who loved adventure, men well-versed in how to handle a gun, how to steal, how to hold their own against others of their kind, men not adverse to furthering their own fortunes by driving cattle across the border and selling them, and men not overly concerned with life itself. In fact, all the accounts of this time impress us with the reckless and casual attitude toward the taking of men's lives and the losing of one's own life. Men courted danger and death itself in an almost debonair manner. No great importance was placed upon dying, and security, which we hear so much about today, was hardly thought of. Compare the man ready to kill or be killed, giving it hardly a thought, with the careful lives of today, the modern seekers of old-age pensions and fringe benefits! Henry and men like Henry hardly went out of their way to dodge danger, so able were they to cope with it. Tough rugged specimens that they were, sleeping on the ground at night with only a blanket or two to cover them, it is hardly conceivable that in a decade they were replaced by the electric-blanket generation.

Henry never had an automobile in his life. He covered thousands of miles during his lifetime on horseback, and everyone agrees that he always owned and rode good horses. If he had to go somewhere faster than a horse could take him, he sometimes took a train. He told one trusted friend, along toward the end of his life, that he guessed he would "buy a car, one of these days," and then added, "for my wife!" However, he never got around to purchasing a car, and when death caught up with him, he had yet to own a car.

At some time during his stay in Mexico, he came into contact with Pancho Villa and served him in some capacity. Villa liked and admired Henry, and later when Henry came to Quemado, someone brought word to him that Villa was inviting him to a celebration he was having in Mexico. Henry left his friends and spent two or three days in Mexico at the party. When he returned he had one thousand dollars in cash plus several other gifts that he claimed Villa had given him.

It is likely that when Henry first went to Mexico, he took the name of Henry Coleman. Anyway, that was the name he used when he first arrived in New Mexico. "It was my understanding that when Henry

was a young man, he went by the name of Street Hudspeth and that his real name was Henry Street Hudspeth," one man told me.[2]

His arrival in New Mexico seems to have been in the nature of the tides of the sea, which come and go, slipping upon the shore in the day and slipping back at night. There is no way of knowing how many times or for what reasons Henry came and went across the border, or how long he stayed at a time. Legend lends its voice to this phase of his life, but not without some degree of authenticity. There were certain incidents to pinpoint his activities, and if these incidents were not entirely accurate, they were based on some degree of truth.

It was frequently mentioned that Henry was a cousin to Ed Cullen, who was killed during a train holdup engineered by Black Jack Ketchum, and that Henry was also related to Ketchum.[3] It is thought that Henry might have slipped across the border from Mexico to help Ketchum and his banditry.

An elderly brand inspector of Catron County named Abe Steele saw Henry in Mexico when both men were working for American cow companies there.[4] Henry had a string of as many as twelve good horses, and Abe noted with appreciation how good they were, how gentle, and that they were freshly branded! The brand on the horses was BX. In telling friends about the incident, Abe wondered why such good horses—a dozen of them—had all been branded at the same time. One of his friends had an idea. He leaned down and drew another brand, 3Λ, in the sand, which was the brand of a ranch in the Sacramento Mountains, and they all figured out then just how Henry had come by that particular bunch of horses.

Henry came back at some time during the 1890s and worked for the G-Bar in Arizona, then went back into Mexico about 1896.[5] It was somewhere around this time that Henry met and befriended a big, powerful young man named Cliff Jenkins.[6] It is speculated that the younger man somehow came to hero-worship the older man, who was wily and wise. Henry could give lots of good advice to Cliff on how to do this and how to do that, and they became friends. Cliff was close to being a professional boxer, but he could not match his older friend with the six-shooter. Henry could pull a gun faster than the eye could see—rattlesnake fast!

One story persists, from different sources, about how Henry got into serious trouble at a bar in Juárez, Mexico, and was thrown in a stockade known as the "bullpen." It was rumored he had even been given a death sentence. Concerned relatives and friends went to Juárez to try to intercede, but things looked bad for Henry. They happened upon Cliff, who naturally wanted to help. Together they engineered a plan by which Cliff would ride up to the outside of the Mexican jail and throw a rope over to Henry and pull him to safety. "Let's send that wild crazy son of a bitch after him," the friends reportedly thought, "and if he gets killed, we won't lose nothing!" So Cliff rode up to the outside of the bullpen and over went the rope. Desperate to escape the prison, Henry grabbed the rope. The bullpen had been constructed with sharp materials on top of the wall to hinder such escapes, and when Cliff spurred his horse to pull Henry to safety, Henry's hand was badly injured. After the incident it was said he could never again completely open his hand. During the attempted escape, the rope was also cut in two and Henry fell back into the bullpen. On top of everything else, some Mexican guards opened fire on Cliff with their rifles. He returned fire but had his horse shot from under him, and he had to race to the Rio Grande on foot. "I was makin' such speed," he said afterward, "that you could've drove a four-horse team and wagon across the river behind me an' they'd have never wet a hair!"

Henry was left to repine in jail, but eventually his friends were able to bribe the authorities and he was released. He joined his young benefactor in the United States, and together they drifted up to around Hillsboro in Sierra County. Old Mexico wasn't a healthy climate for them anymore.

Some accounts of Henry paint a picture of a tense, serious, unsmiling man, but this image was touched up in brighter tones by one man who knew him. "Henry laughed a lot, and he liked a good joke as much as anybody," he told me. "He'd play pranks along with the best of them." In fact, he told me about one of these pranks, which Henry planned and perpetrated near Deming. Some of Henry's friends, and conceivably Henry himself on occasion, had one pastime that proved both profitable and entertaining. They would ride across the border into Old Mexico and steal lots of cattle—usually steers—and drive them back into New Mexico, up to Deming, and ship them out from there.[7] One day when Henry and four or five others were loafing around town, they hatched up the idea that it would be very funny and amusing to dress themselves up to resemble the Apache Kid and some of his warriors.[8] This warrior was still in the country at the time and was making occasional raiding forays. Henry's plan was to feather up himself and his friends, follow their acquaintances into Mexico, and station themselves where they could be seen by the rustlers when they neared the border with their stolen cattle. This they did, and since it must be concluded that they had been on a few of these expeditions themselves, they knew only too well the trail the raiders would be taking, and where would be the most expedient point to apprehend them.

Imagine the consternation of the men with the newly and painstakingly acquired herd upon seeing half a dozen Indian warriors bearing down on them in the distance. Jumpy as they were over the possibility that the Mexican owners of the cattle might have struck their trail, the complication of having a clash with the Apaches was too rich for their blood! They took flight to escape as best they could. Henry's strategy was to send about half of his "warriors" after them, to keep them running. He and the others took over the cattle and brought them along their destined way at a safe distance. The pursuers put enough fear in the duped rustlers so that they made a good getaway and went into temporary hiding. Then the "braves," who presumably had some other attire cached along the way, brought the twice-stolen bunch of cattle into Deming and shipped them.

Hearing about this frisky episode made me wonder whether Henry was the type who could sometimes be found with "a bunch of the boys," whooping it up down at the old saloon. Did he follow the old pattern of subsisting on beans and black coffee when he was out on a roundup and then become a product of undiluted alcohol when he hit town? "Henry'd take a drink," his friend told me, "but you never saw him drunk. He always knew what he was doing. Nobody ever caught him off guard." Henry's mind, apparently, remained on sentry duty around the clock. He was always on the alert; his reflexes much have been on a par with those of some creature of the wild.

Notes

1. Coleman may have been in close contact with his brother, Lee, who was ranching at Sonora, Texas, until he moved to Douglas, Arizona, in 1936. Claude Hudspeth to Jerry Thompson, email, June 16, 2021, editor's files.
2. Coleman is enumerated on the 1870 census in Marion County, Arkansas, as "Street" and thereafter in the census as "Henry."
3. There is no evidence Coleman was related to Cullen or Ketchum. Three hardened criminals—Ed "Shoot-em-up Dick" Cullen, "Black Jack" Ketchum, and Dave Atkins—robbed the US Post Office and the railroad station at Steins Peak, twenty miles west of Lordsburg, New Mexico, on December 9, 1897. At gunpoint they boarded the Southern Pacific train

and gave orders to proceed down the tracks to where two bonfires had been torched by accomplices Tom Ketchum and Will Carner. As the train screeched to a halt, a gun battle erupted with guards in the express car; Ed Cullen was hit in the head with buckshot and killed. "Boys, I am dead," were said to have been his last words. Cullen was buried in an unmarked grave at Shakespeare near Lordsburg. "Ed 'Shoot-Em-Up Dick' Cullen," *Find a Grave*, accessed October 5, 2020, https://www.findagrave.com/memorial/45111161/ed-cullen; Bob Alexander, *Lawmen, Outlaws and S.O.Bs.*, vol. 2, *Gunfighters of the Old Southwest* (Silver City, NM: High Lonesome Books, 2007); Bob Boze Bell, "The Blast at Steins Pass," *True West Magazine*, July 15, 2014, https://truewestmagazine.com/article/the-blast-at-steins-pass/, accessed July 3, 2022.

Thomas Edward "Black Jack" Ketchum and Henry Coleman had a lot in common. Ketchum was born in San Saba, Texas, in 1863, came west as a young man, and worked on a number of ranches in New Mexico, including the Bell Ranch. Ketchum joined the famous Hole in the Wall Gang and robbed a number of trains, stores, and post offices in southern Colorado and northeastern New Mexico Territory. After he single-handedly attempted to rob a train near Folsom, New Mexico, in August 1899, he was shot and captured. Taken to Clayton in Union County, New Mexico, he was found guilty and hanged on April 26, 1901. The hanging went badly and Black Jack was decapitated. Postcards of lawmen posing with the truncated head and torso were sold throughout the Southwest. Jeffrey Burton, *The Deadliest Outlaws: The Ketchum Gang and the Wild Bunch* (Denton: University of North Texas Press, 2009); Tony Hillerman, *The Great Taos Bank Robbery and Other Indian Country Affairs* (Albuquerque: University of New Mexico Press, 1973); Clark Secrest, "'Black Jack Died Game': The Bandit Career of Thomas E. Ketchum," *Colorado Heritage Magazine* 30, no. 4 (2000). See also, "Thomas E. Ketchum," *Colorado Encyclopedia*, accessed July 3, 2022. https://coloradoencyclopedia.org/article/thomas-e-ketchum.

4. Albert Steele was born in Missouri on December 27, 1879. He died at age 59 in Datil, New Mexico, on December 3, 1937, and was buried in the Magdalena Cemetery. Steele came west as a young man and worked for the Frank Hubbell Cattle and Sheep Company and several other ranches for several years before he became the manager of the large V-Cross-T Ranch. From 1913 to 1915, prior to becoming cattle inspector at Datil, Steele said he trailed as many as fifty-four thousand head of cattle to Magdalena. There is no indication Steele was ever married. Fourteenth

Census (1920), Socorro County, NM, and 15th Census (1930), Catron County, NM; *Catron County News* (Quemado, NM), December 10, 1937; "Steele World War I Draft Registration Card," ancestry.com, accessed October 8, 2020.

5. The G-Bar Ranch, or Gold Bar Ranch, is in the foothills of the Muskhog Mountains in Cochise County, northwest of Wilcox, Arizona.

6. Cliff Jenkins is the fictitious name the author uses for "Salty" John Cox.

7. Short notations of Henry Coleman shipping large numbers of cattle from the Deming stockyards are common in the Deming newspapers of the era. For example, see *Deming Headlight*, May 18, 1901, and *Deming Graphic*, December 18, 1906.

8. The Apache Kid (Hasjat-bay-nag-ntay, meaning "brave," "tall," and "he who will come to a mysterious end") was born in 1860 in Aravaipa Canyon, twenty-five miles south of the San Carlos Reservation in southeastern Arizona. He became a respected scout for the army and then a renegade. Following a court-martial for mutiny and desertion, he was sentenced to ten years in Alcatraz but was freed in 1888, only to be rearrested and sentenced to seven years in the Arizona Territorial Prison at Yuma. Following a gun battle at Globe, Arizona, he escaped into the desert. There were many alleged sightings of the Apache Kid in the years that followed. The last crime connected to the Apache Kid was in the San Mateo Mountains southwest of Socorro, New Mexico, a result of which was that Charles Anderson and a posse of cowboys allegedly killed the Kid high in the mountains. One mile from Apache Kid Peak in the Apache Kid Wilderness in the Cibola National Forest, a stone monument marks the alleged grave of the Kid, although evidence indicates he was never buried, and coyote-ravaged bones and shreds of the Kid's clothing could be seen for years. His head was on display at the mining town of Chloride, Arizona, as late as 1907. Cattlemen in western New Mexico continued to blame the Apache Kid for rustling as late as the 1930s. Jess G. Hayes, *Apache Vengeance: The True Story of the Apache Kid* (Albuquerque: University of New Mexico Press, 1954); Ben Camp and J. C. Dykes, *Cow Dust and Saddle Leather* (Norman: University of Oklahoma Press, 1968); and Phyllis de la Garza, *The Apache Kid* (Tucson: Westerlore Press, 1995). For the most recent scholarship, see Paul Andrew Hutton, *The Apache Wars: The Apache Kid, the Hunt for Geronimo, and the Captive Boy Who Started the Longest War in American History* (New York: Crown, 2016).

Chapter 3

Homesteading

I t was about 1909 that Henry turned up around Quemado with a wife whom he had acquired in the Deming country. Clara was her name—a dark and wiry woman described as showing to have a good deal of Indian blood.[1] From this time on, the number of first-hand accounts of Henry's activities challenges the pen to keep them straight.

When Henry and Clara first came to the country, they lived out toward Salt Lake from Quemado, on what was known as the old Record place. It was on the lower Largo Creek, not far from Nation's Draw. If a man did well in that rigorous country in those days, he had to be an opportunist of the most resourceful kind. Henry was that. He worked for wages some of the time, while he and Clara built up their new holdings by any and all available means. Quemado proved to be a fruitful field for their efforts.

In 1914 Henry and one Walter J. Hutchinson filed an application for water rights on the lower Largo Creek, or Rito Creek as it was called at that time.[2] Their plan was to build a dam across a narrow, rocky part of the streambed. They went to a prodigious amount of work, using teams and scrapers, and constructed their dam to catch the floodwaters of the higher country to the south. They intended to use this harnessed water for irrigation purposes. But for all their labors, the dam washed out under the pressure of one of the roaring floods that came during the rainy season.

Not long after Henry came to the country, his friend Cliff Jenkins came along after him to try his luck, and Henry and Cliff had a falling out. No one is quite sure why they came to a disagreement. There might have been a number of reasons. One theory is that the two started stealing from one another. But that theory was discounted by one acquaintance who said that as far as he knew, the men were never too friendly after Cliff went back to Hillsboro to steal a herd of horses for himself. There was a ranch near Hillsboro that had some good horses. Some say that a bank had a judgment on the ranch and the horses were really owned by the bank. Cliff wanted to go back and get some of the horses, but Henry did not think this was such a good idea.

"If you want those horses," he told Cliff, "We'll send somebody down there to buy them." But Cliff did not take his advice. He went down to the ranch and drove the horses up to the Quemado country. Just why the two men would be so bitter against each other over this the relater of the tale did not fully understand, but he said they never liked each other after that. At the time they were both working for a big cattle company and were out with the roundup wagon. A certain known gunman arrived at the wagon one day and it was thought he might have been sent up to kill Cliff. But, as it turned out, he and Cliff became good friends, and it was [the gunman] Sewell and Henry who did not get along.[3]

Eventually, they had a quarrel and Sewell tried to draw a gun on Henry, but before his hand could even get near his holster, Henry's gun was out and aimed at him. Flushed with anger and embarrassment, Sewell reined his horse away and rode off. Henry figured there would be another showdown, and this is one of those cases where I was given two slightly different versions of the same basic facts.

Said one man,

Henry and I was bed partners. We shared the same bedroll.
We was pickin' a place for our bed one evening, and Henry threw
down his gun belt and covered it with a tarp so that just the end
of the holster and part of the belt showed. Henry had taken the
gun out and had it hid under his sweater that he had on, but he
just wanted to see how anxious Sewell might be to catch him
unarmed. We was watching Sewell, and when he come in, he
sure enough did notice that part of that belt stickin' out from
under the tarp, and he edged around and tried to check on it to
see if the gun was in that holster. When he found it wasn't in
there, he knew that Henry was on to him and would be ready for
him no matter what he tried to do, so he left the outfit soon after
that. He knew he'd come out second best, or was liable to.

The other version was polished to a little higher sheen. Said
this man,

Henry was workin' for the K-outfit and he and Bill Hinton slept
in the same bedroll.[4] And Henry thought there was a feller there
that wanted to kill him, so he unstrapped his big Colt and left it in
his holster, and stuck it under the bed, where it could be seen just
a little. An' he told Bill, 'Now, if he tries to kill me. I'll get him
with this little forty-one Derringer, an' that son of a bitch will
be just as dead as if I used my gun on him!' But you know, that
feller must have known that Henry was ready for him, because
he never did try anything.

As to the horses that Cliff brought up from Hillsboro: he got word
that they had been missed and that the owners had a pretty good idea
of where they were. So he took them over into Arizona. I wondered
aloud whether he might have wanted to sell them over there but was
told that he didn't, that Cliff was using the horses at home, and that
he liked a certain horse so much that he probably figured on bringing
them back sooner or later and using them right there. But while the
search was on, the horse pasture of a good friend across the state line
seemed like a pretty good haven.

Someone was doing some informing, because a member of the New Mexico Sanitary Board came in on horseback, hot on the trail of the missing horses.[5] Could it have been Henry Coleman, who was by now Cliff's hated enemy? "It takes a thief to catch a thief"—so goes the old adage. But it is doubtful whether Henry would have bothered with this kind of retribution; he had plenty of business of his own to attend to. The man from the Sanitary Board proved to be quite a tracker. He rode straight to the horse pasture in question, where the horses were peacefully grazing. At a nearby house, there was an almost obvious absence of anyone in sight, and no one ever showed. The man cut out the horses and took them back to the Hillsboro country where they came from—that is, all but one. This one was a horse who was such a pet and so well liked by his abductor that rather than lose him, Cliff took him to an isolated spot, shot him, and then burned the carcass. Just how sentimental was he, anyway?

Notes

1. Clara Coleman's tombstone at the small Sacred Heart Cemetery in Quemado indicates she was born Jennie Clarintha Barber in October 1875 in Llano County, Texas. Her name was actually Clarintha Potter, and she was the daughter of Warren Potter and Sophia Ellender Choat. Clara had an older half-sister, Nancy, from her mother's first marriage to Green K. Hokit, a Confederate veteran of Burnett's 1st Battalion of Texas Sharpshooters. It is from Henry Coleman's recollection that Clara had a sister named Theresia (Thersa or Teresia) living in Lohn, in McCulloch County, Texas, that Clara's lineage can be traced. Her father was a sergeant in a regiment of New York infantry during the Civil War. In 1879 Warren Potter established the small community of Apex at the head of Cold Creek, eight miles southwest of Cherokee in southwestern San Saba County, where he served as justice of the peace and postmaster. Apex never had a population of more than twenty people, and the post office in the Potter home had so few patrons, it was discontinued after only a year and the mail directed to Field Creek. At Apex Potter was able to acquire 320 acres, 30 acres of which he farmed. He then purchased an additional 640 acres from the Gulf,

Colorado and Santa Fe Railroad. Within a few years, Potter had also bought half interest in a much larger ranch of 5,716 acres on which he grazed some 1,607 livestock. Potter was deeply in debt, however, and when he died in 1887, his portion of the large ranch was auctioned off on the steps of the San Saba County courthouse on June 7, 1887. How Clara met Henry Coleman has not been determined with any certainty. Moreover, a marriage certificate has not been located for Clara and Henry, in either Texas or New Mexico, and it is probable that they were never married. When Henry was 30 and Clara was 26, they appear on the 1900 census at Deming, New Mexico, living on Gold Avenue, the main north-south artery in the small community. According to the census, the couple had been married for five years. Clara is also listed on the 1910 census with Henry at their small homestead four miles north of Quemado. She gave her age at the time as 35. She died "an untimely death," the tombstone reads, on December 11, 1918. During the latter part of her life, Clara's Alabama-born mother lived with the younger sister, Teresia, at Lohn, Texas, and died there at the age of 69 on January 26, 1932. Theresia Bates died at the age of 73 at Lohn on April 24, 1949. Tenth Census (1880), San Saba County, TX; 12th Census (1900), Luna County, NM; 13th Census (1910), Socorro County, NM; *San Saba* (TX) *News*, February 14, 1880, and May 4, May 27, and October 7, 1887; Alice Gray Upchurch, "Apex, TX," *Handbook of Texas Online*, accessed June 1, 2021, https://www.tshaonline.org/handbook/entries/apex-tx.

2. Texas-born, 21-year-old Walter J. Hutchinson is enumerated on the 1910 census as Coleman's hired hand at Coleman's 160-acre homestead north of Quemado. Fifty-five-year-old Ben Hutchinson, probably his father, was also working for Coleman at the time. Fifteenth Census (1920), Socorro County, NM.

3. Sewell may be a fictitious name.

4. Bill Hinton cannot be identified with any certainty.

5. The New Mexico Livestock Board is the oldest law enforcement agency in New Mexico. Although New Mexico did not become a state until 1912, the Livestock Board had been formed as early as 1887 as the Cattle Sanitary Board. The Sheep Sanitary Board was created two years later. In northeast New Mexico, the Northern New Mexico Stock Growers Association had preceded the Sanitary Board. The two organizations, the Cattle Sanitary Board and the Sheep Sanitary Board, merged in 1967. See New Mexico Livestock Board website, https://www.nmlbonline.com/, accessed February 9, 2021.

Chapter 4

Shenanigans

A gainst the constancy of the piñon-studded mesas, the brooding blue of the higher hills, and the wide yellow reaches of the open country that connects to the blue and purple mountains in panoramic continuity rode Henry Coleman. Against all this changeless natural beauty, man has always capered across the stage and has always felt the need to compromise the setting with his little antics; he must make history, no matter what! In the plateau country of western New Mexico, the rabbit brush gives up its pleasantly stringent odor after a rain; jay birds cackle in their flight; winds turn the silver side of the cottonwood trees to sight in the summer and claw cruelly at the earth with icy talons in the spring. And with all these seasonal rulings carried out to the letter for hundreds of years on end, the explosive little goings-on of men seem to lash out at the natural world and pit us in opposition. The more civilized the man, the more he seems like a trespasser, changing the face of the country where he resides, or passes through.

At this time and in this country of which I write, there seemed to be historical patterns. The Spanish American people living in little communities and running their cattle not too far outside the towns were, for the most part, peaceful and home loving. An old-time rancher once said that while it was true that everyone had to steal a few cattle to keep even in the days of the open range, still the gringos far out-stole the Spanish Americans. The latter were too easygoing and not inclined to be suspicious. The gringo pioneer ranchers, on the other hand, were "rimmers" and hardy opportunists. The Spanish Americans did not want trouble and were hard working and remained at home with their families. And that is where they lost out, because the zealous white men apparently did not mind prowling in the moonlight to add a few stolen cattle to their herds. They were more restless, more apt to follow up the sight they had seen the previous day of two cows up some draw with newborn calves that could be carried off and raised on an old milk cow, or a big maverick with a hide just begging to be branded.

But most ordinary ranchers did not steal on a big scale. All added up together—the gringo ranchers and the communal-living Spanish Americans—the resulting sum was a fairly gentle-hued pattern, where browns and blacks and whites and light tan shades blended, for the most part, without clashing. Across this blending pattern zigzagged the ramblings and connivings and bold moves of Henry Coleman like an alien scarlet thread, standing out against the quieter colors, streaking across them, and in places exploding into splotches of loud-colored activity, like a stellar photograph of whirling multicolored nebula in space.

Where someone else might take one or two head of cattle, Henry would steal by the dozen. He was a promoter by nature, a diplomat with people, likable, observant, and good, so good, with a gun. With his nice personality and his command of Spanish, he quickly made friends with the Spanish-speaking people around Quemado. He was welcomed in their homes, and he soon knew a lot about them—their comings and goings and what livestock they had. He had his special friends among the Spanish people; he liked Spanish food, and there was one kitchen that he liked to frequent for its delicious enchiladas and other dishes.

But soon, strange things started happening in the area around Quemado. Twenty head of cattle at a time, or even more, would unaccountably disappear. Henry seemed to always be on the move, a man of constant and stealthy activity. No doubt his driving energy was one of the big factors in his various and sundry projects. He was not a man to sit by the fireside; the mainspring in Henry was too tightly wound; he was restless and ambitious. His active mind, capable of promoting all kinds of schemes, seemed never to be at rest.

The Quemado terrain was particularly vulnerable to his operations. The easygoing populace, for the most part, was not accustomed to watching for nightriders, or constantly checking on their cattle and horses. The country was largely open, with a few water holes and horse pastures fenced off. To keep up with Henry, it would have taken constant "rimming," and the people around Quemado were used to easier ways of handling livestock. A stray cow with an unbranded calf might turn up miles away, and a good neighbor would send word that he had her, or would put the right brand on the calf and then tell someone to inform the owner. That was the ideal way, and there are instances related to Henry's doing this very thing, in good neighborly fashion, at least for the people he liked. Legend has it, however, that he neglected to notify the owners in many cases, and not only did he neglect to tell them, but near where he lived, cattle started disappearing in large numbers. As one old-timer said, "None of them fellers ever denied stealin'. They'd laugh about it, and Henry told me one time that he'd stole more cattle than he'd ever own. But he wasn't the only one."

No, not the only one, but quite an operation at that! Henry, it turned out, had a good friend at Zuni, and this friend had a contract to furnish beef for the Zuni Indians, who were government wards. So signs of cattle being trailed in that direction became common. There were a lot of missing cattle in the Quemado region. "At first," one rancher told me, "Henry just took them up there and they butchered them out and disposed of the brands. So if he was able to get them up there and not be apprehended, he didn't leave no evidence." Later it was rumored that he started showing even more bravado. "He took them to Zuni," the man said, "but instead of butchering them right away, he got to branding them out and letting them run up there." This left loopholes. Henry did not apparently see the need for so much continued caution, and gradually, the ones who were looking for evidence were able in this way to build up their case. Eventually, a few of these cattle were found.

Chapter 5

On the Zuni Trail

Nor were his northern outlets apparently confined to Zuni; there was a wheeler-dealer butcher or two near Gallup and others who were implicated. Likewise, it appeared to often be in a two-way deal; cattle from the Quemado region would go north, and there might be a bunch of Indian cattle or horses coming south on the return trip. Henry quite evidently knew how to steal the cattle, how and when to take them the way that tracks would be hardest to follow, and how to dispose of them at the northern and southern terminus. He is said to have operated so deftly that the Natives of the country hardly knew what was happening. They were in the habit of earmarking their cattle early, then branding them later. Henry would reportedly get these earmarked cattle, brand them, and work over the earmarks. When the local folk had been fleeced pretty badly, they woke up to find that the situation was serious. If they protested or tried to interfere with Henry, they knew their lives were in danger. I asked one old-timer why, when cattle can only be driven fifteen miles or so in a day, people would not have watched Henry and then followed up when they noticed a lot of fresh tracks. "Well," he mused, "the country was awful big an' they wasn't used to things like that. They only worked their cattle about once a year." And, he added, bringing out the fact that nearly everyone attested to, "they were afraid to mess with Henry."

Henry's mode of travel was of special interest to me. Depending solely upon a horse for transportation, as he did, what was his technique of travel? I was told that he usually drove along a couple of extra horses and packed a small amount of camp equipment. He liked to change mounts, and he usually had a bedroll along. A little paint pack mule carried his bed. This little beast of burden always trotted along right behind Henry, no matter what gait he struck. He would pack his bed on her and then turn her loose. She did not have to be led or driven; she just followed along directly behind him. Henry could go from Mexico to Canada in this manner if he wanted to.

He was a lone wolf in some respects; still, he had help when he needed it. He always had assistance when driving cattle for any distance. One of the most faithful and dependable employees was Ben Foster, an old fellow as tough as they came, who reputedly specialized in doing lots of Henry's dirty work for him.[1] Gray-haired, said some, but a gunman and a cow thief from way back. His name comes bouncing on the scene again and again; he performed in a kind of a catalytic capacity. In adventure after adventure, incident upon incident, appears the name of Ben Foster, the ever ready and dispensable "Man Friday," filling in here and there, always on the spot when needed, but a fast fader when circumstance decreed! Henry apparently had what could be termed as a ring of operators, with Ben Foster coming on stage frequently and in every capacity. Henry was the brains, the one who laid the plans and whose sharp mind allowed him to elude the detection of his activities with great skill and ingenuity. One elderly rancher stated that some honest men helped Henry—some through ignorance, some through fear, and some just because they liked the man and were his friend. He could take a bunch of cattle on a long drive, stop along the way with friends, and be fed and have a place to sleep.

Henry was careful not to offend the wrong people. Then, too, men prided themselves in those days in keeping information private. The present-day art of "informing" was not admired, either for a price or in itself. If a man and his family happened to like Henry, it would have been almost impossible for a lawman to find out anything about Henry from that man or from his family. A good example of how men practiced this principle in those days was the success that Billy the Kid had, for a long time, in hiding out with his different friends. And Henry Coleman had his friends, too.

Besides, Henry was truly a paradox and an enigma. On the one hand comes a tale of unparalleled toughness and brutality; on the other comes a story, equally authentic, of Henry, the good and kindly neighbor. He might easily have had a genuinely dual personality, since it is a known fact that such personalities do exist. The comparisons of different episodes in the life of Henry Coleman defy one another in disparity.

Here sits one old-timer, with a sadly reminiscent look in his eyes. "I hate to tell you this story," he says, apologetically. "I've known so many men that liked Henry; I liked him myself, but, well, that's the way it happened." The story concerned Henry's storekeeping friend in Zuni.

This man traded groceries and dry goods to Indians on the Zuni reservation, and he often took cattle in payment.[2] In them days the Indians didn't know too much English; maybe the storekeeper did his trading in the Zuni language or used sign language. And the Indians really didn't have no one to represent them in their trading, no one who knew right from wrong and saw to it that they got a square deal. It was the same old story of the white man cheating the Indian! The Indians didn't know the value of what they had to trade, and that storekeeper, he took advantage of all this. He gave them prices for their cows that was just ridiculous. Why, hell, he'd give them as little as four or five dollars a head!

He made arrangements with Henry to drive the cattle away once he traded for them—to drive them a good long distance, to be pastured. Henry would take them back to the country around Quemado, where he was living then. On one of these trips, he just could not resist picking up a few extra Indian cattle—ten or twelve head.

The Indians, perhaps from sad experience, missed their cattle and picked up the trail. When Henry reached home, it was along toward evening and too late to put the cattle where he was intending to keep them, so he just threw them all into the corral. Next morning when he got up, there was four Indians down by the corral, looking over them cattle. They all wore their hair in big knots at the back of their heads, tied with bright ribbons. They had maybe been up all night on the way. Henry thought fast.

"Cook up some more breakfast," he told Clara. "Plenty more! We'll feed 'em, and while they're eatin', you slip down there to the corral and cut out those extras and drive 'em off."

Clara did what she was told. The Indians were invited inside. Henry greeted them real friendly-like; he gave them to understand that if any of their cattle had gotten in with his bunch, by mistake, he'd see about them, and in the meantime, they were to come and eat. The Indians were very hungry and they ate a lot. They were probably thinking what a good feller Henry was, and how they'd get them cattle and go back to Zuni, an' everything was going to be all right. Henry saw to it that breakfast dragged out as long as he could make it. They ate a big lot an' they visited. Finally, they sauntered back to the corral.

"Now, which cattle was it you was talkin' about?" says Henry. The Indians climbed up on the corral poles to point them out. But the only cattle in the corral was them ones that Henry had got from the storekeeper; them others was long gone, them that Clara had drove off. The Indians knew then what had happened. They got mad and they stormed at Henry. But they didn't know what they was up against. At about the time that they had been asked in to eat, someone working for Henry had been told to take two ropes down the corral and put 'em in the water barrel.

As previously mentioned, wells in those days were nearly all hand dug, and were for house use, nearly altogether. A windmill pumped the water up, and it ran through a little pipe into a barrel. Water for the house was carried from the barrel in buckets. That was the usual setup, and it was the water system used by the Colemans.

The narrator went on:

The ropes was in this barrel, an' they had been soakin' all through breakfast. You know, a wet rope is quite a weapon—it sure is! The Indians, they got pretty damn mad, an' they come toward Henry, threatenin'-like. Looked like they thought flat the four of them could handle him. He was just standing there right by the water barrel, an' he didn't have no gun on, that they could see. When the first one got up pretty close, Henry moved like lightnin', an' he drew out one of them wet ropes from that barrel an' conked that first Indian over the head with it an' laid him out cold. The rest was comin' on, and Henry got every one of them, an' he worked them all over with that rope, and they was lyin' around there on the ground, like a bunch of picnickers on a Sunday afternoon!

I tell you, that Henry, he could fight any way that anyone wanted to; with a gun he could shoot cans in the air all day long and never miss one, and if a man wanted to fight with his fists, why Henry could do that too. And he could jump and hit a man in the chest with both his feet at once, and it was like being kicked by a mule. You wouldn't believe that, would you? Well, now, he sure could!

After a spell, them Indians, they started coming to. They'd open their eyes an' rub their old heads, an' got up. But there wasn't no more fight in any of 'em. They went outside of the corral to where their horses was tied an' they left. When they got back to the reservation, they went an' looked up the storekeeper an' told him what had happened. He didn't give them no satisfaction. He just said, well it was better not to fool with Coleman, an' he said he'd pay 'em for what cattle they'd lost—the usual price, an' let's just forget about it!

Another tale that shows the venom of which Henry was capable can still be attested to by standing evidence in the form of an old fence line—miles of it—out north of Quemado. This fence was once on what was known as the Nations Ranch holdings.[3] When it was first built and new, it strongly irked Henry. For some reason he did not want it, but he just couldn't stand the idea of that fence line. So what he did was cut every wire, for miles, between every post! That in itself was a long, hard job. It was generally known that Henry did that, although I do not know whether the Nations outfit ever proved it in court or tried to get after Henry about it. Today the fence is still sanding, and the wires are spliced at every point where he had cut them.

Notes

1. Very little information is available on Ben Foster. He does not appear on the 1900, 1910, or 1920 US Census and may have died in Mexico as the author indicates.
2. Zuni trader Edward Vanderwagen and Zuni cattleman William Herbert Bosson, both of whom paid Henry Coleman with checks for cattle, were issued subpoenas in the larceny trial of George W. Henderson in the March 1920 term of district court in Socorro. The district attorney, Fred Nicholas, had decided to try Henderson separately since Coleman could not be apprehended. Vanderwagen and Bosson World War I Draft Registration Cards, ancestry.com, accessed July 20, 2021; 15th (1920) and 16th Census (1930), McKinley County, NM; Subpoenas, Vanderwagen and Bosson, January 14, 1920, Eleanor Williams Papers, in possession of Helen Cress (hereafter cited as Williams Papers).
3. Joseph Henry Nations, well-known stockman and businessman of El Paso, Texas, was born in Gonzales County, Texas, on January 5, 1857, the son of Eli Nations and Eliza Woodruff. Nations's half-sister was the wife of Anson Jones, fourth president of the Republic of Texas and a proponent of Texas annexation to the United States. Working as a cowboy for fifty cents a day as a teenager, Nations, by the age of 18, had enough money to buy a small herd of cattle that he drove from Gonzales to the Gulf Coast, where he ranched for several years. Nations married Ida Mae Hicks of Moulton in Lavaca County, Texas, in October 1880, and the couple raised four daughters. In 1882 Nations moved with his father to Presidio County in the Texas Big Bend and ranched there until 1897, when he sold out and established a ranch near Midland and a second ranch in Pecos County. The couple

moved permanently to El Paso in the winter of 1887. In 1906–1907 Nations acquired a large sheep ranch in what became known as Nations Draw north of Quemado, drilling wells to ensure additional grazing for his ever-expanding herds of sheep and cattle. The Nations Land and Cattle Company experienced a boom during World War I, but the rapid influx of settlers into the area during the war appears to have acerbated animosities between Hispanics and Anglos. Many of the Texans held deeply rooted racial prejudices against anyone of Hispanic ancestry. There was also conflict between homesteaders and the larger ranchers. Incidents of rustling and violence became common. As noted by Williams, Henry Coleman was accused of cutting one of the Nations' fences.

While he was in El Paso, Nations became owner of the J. H. Nations Meat and Supply Company, one of the more prosperous businesses in the Southwest, located in a large building in the Nations block in the heart of the El Paso business district. He also invested in real estate in east El Paso and helped develop several neighborhoods. By 1914 Nations had as many as fifteen thousand head of livestock in the El Paso and Pecos Counties in Texas, as well as the Socorro and Valencia Counties in New Mexico. The collapse of cattle prices in a worldwide depression after the war ruined many of the small ranchers in western Socorro County and even larger landowners such as Nations. The Nations Land and Cattle Company was unable to survive a second depression from 1920 to 1923, and two years later the company folded and Frank A. Hubbell Sr. acquired the company's deeded and leased properties.

There is a lone grave of a man killed by a Nations gunman for trying to water his horse at a stock tank at a place called Horse Camp, north of Quemado. Other similar graves dot the landscape. Although Nations's New Mexico cowboys could be ruthless, Nations had a reputation in El Paso of being a "most generous and benevolent man" who had a standing offer to "supply meat free to the worthy poor." Nations died in El Paso on November 27, 1929. Nations Draw, encompassing a large area north of Quemado, is generally referred to today as Hubbell's Draw after Frank Hubbell. Fifteenth Census (1920), El Paso, El Paso County, TX; Patrick Hogan, *Prehistoric Settlement Patterns in West-Central New Mexico: The Fence Lake Coal Lease Surveys* (Albuquerque: University of New Mexico Office of Contract Archeology, 1985), 13–28; B. B. Paddock, *History and*

Biographical Record of North and Western Texas, vol. 2 (Chicago: Lewis Publishing, 1906); Harwood P. Hinton, *History of the Cattlemen of Texas: A Brief Resume of the Live Stock Industry of the Southwest and a Biographical Sketch of Many of the Important Characters Whose Lives are Interwoven Therein*, DeGolyer Library Cowboy and Ranch Life Series 1 (repr., Austin: Texas State Historical Association, 1991); Martin Donell Kohout, "Joseph Henry Nations," *Handbook of Texas Online*, accessed September 7, 2021, http://www.tshaonnline.rog/about/people/martin-kohout.

Chapter 6

Outlaw Born too Late

I n any country there are always the braggers—the tough boys who do most of their bravest deeds while sitting around a campfire and telling about it. One such blustering hero was with one of the old J L wagons near Mangas. For several days this man had been regaling the other men with tales of his big exploits. Among other things he claimed to have known Henry Coleman and backed him down on several occasions. No doubt the other boys were pretty well fed up on all this campfire bravado and were wishing that someone would shut him up. Their wishes materialized when Henry rode up one evening. He dismounted and rolled a cigarette, the eyes noted for their steely challenge scanning the faces around the fire. When his eyes came to the champ, they stopped and narrowed. The man paled visibly, and it was quite evident, all right, that the two had met before. Henry wasted no words. "Get your horse and get the hell out of here!" Henry told him. His pearl-handled Frontier model Colt hung low down, near his right hip, and everyone knew what could have happened if the man had refused to go. But he went, leaving the shattered remains of all his tall tales behind him, visible only in a faint smile on a tanned face here and there around the fire.

Not always did Henry choose to be so unrelentingly tough. In some instances he gave in with surprising submissiveness. Such as the time when a man named Gonzales came across Henry driving a fair-sized bunch of cattle he had gathered and was taking to his Zuni holding trap. Among the herd were some of Gonzales's cattle. He went and tried to get some help to cut them out, but no one would help him. His anger made him brave, so he went into the bunch lone-handed and cut the cattle out and drove them home. Henry paid no more attention to him than if he had never seen him.

I have two versions of a story about some cattle stolen from the Largo Valley. According to one man, there was a fellow who lived on the Largo and was generous to a fault. Henry had other friends who vouched for him just as strongly. Others spoke strongly, but it was not in favor of Henry. You might say to one man, "Did you ever know Henry Coleman?" and he would tell you stories that praised him; another man, in answer to the same query, might snort and say shortly, "He was a damn snake."

On the debit side of the ledger comes the story of a man who was just a young boy when Henry was at the height of all his activities in the Largo sector. "I was about 12 years old," he recounted, "and one day when I was riding in my dad's pasture, I come up on forty or fifty head of strange horses that I had never seen before." They had "been thrown into a little dry lakebed right in the middle of one of our pastures and were grazing there. The lakebed was hidden from view in almost every direction; anyone had to ride right on to it to see what was in there. It startled me, because I knew there wasn't a human in sight. I set there an' watched them a while, but I knew better than to go snooping around. I went on home, an' next day the horses were gone. They had been taken out in the night." This incident had all the earmarks of a Coleman-Foster job. When things like that were seen, there wasn't too much guesswork about it.

There is a story of the theft that was pinned on Henry. Great pains were taken to apprehend him, but in the end the thief turned out to be someone else. The man most interested in catching Henry at that time was his one-time friend Cliff Jenkins. Cliff would have given a lot to catch Henry red-handed, and he thought his chance had come.

Some ranches near the Arizona line were visited one day by Cliff Jenkins and some companions who were, so they thought, hot on the trail of Henry Coleman. Two horses had just been stolen near the line on the New Mexico side, and, as they were very good horses, the owners took a dim view of their loss. The thief had struck out for the state line. Once over in Arizona, he could take refuge in what they called the "innocent purchaser" law. The law provided protection for the thief. If the outlaw could just sell the stock and get the money, the State of Arizona had a law, at that time, that held that if anyone should unknowingly buy stolen stock, either cattle or horses, he could keep them. If stock was found in his possession and he had already paid for them, they could not be taken away from him. The law might be able to get some of the money they were worth out of someone, but the animals themselves could not be arrested. This little posse was, to a man, panting to apprehend Henry before he crossed the state line. One of the younger men in the party could track almost on a lope. He'd see a track here and a track there, a little piece of snow or a rock disturbed in another place. There never was an Indian who could track any better or faster than he could.

When the horses disappeared, their loss came to light right away and the consensus of opinion almost automatically shouted out the name of the thief—Henry Coleman! They were wrong this time, but the hunt was on, and with added zest because they thought they had Henry in a trap. A light snow aided the tracking and the trail led to the southwest. Word was sent ahead to almost every community of any size to be on the lookout. So it was that the man who stole the horses unwittingly rode right into Clifton, Arizona, where he doubt-less intended to sell them. But authorities were waiting for him, the horses were seized, and the man was arrested. Great was the chagrin of the eager posse because this man had the wrong name. Henry, the canny operator, was not to be so easily trapped.

Perhaps the fame of Henry's trigger finger accounted for a lot of his apparent immunity. Abe Steele, the old band inspector, related another story of Henry's character when he was cornered. This happened during the winter of 1909, at which time Abe was working for the V+T Ranch. He was riding on the San Agustin Plains. There were several inches of snow on the ground when he came across the trail of some cattle. The trail being as fresh as it was, he was able to overtake them within a few miles. Henry Coleman and some young fellow were with the cattle. "Abe, you know I wouldn't steal from the V+T," Henry said. But as they rode along, Abe spotted a couple of bulls carrying the V+T brand, and so he rode into the bunch and cut them out.

Since it was closer to the Slash J L Ranch than to his camp, Abe went into headquarters that evening. The ranch belonged to J. W. Cox. There were two men who were named John Cox in the county, but they were no relation to one another. J. W. Cox was called "Slash J. L." The other man was called "Salty" John Cox, because he lived near Salt Lake.[1] That same evening the marshal rode in, accompanied by a deputy. John Cox told Abe that these fellows were looking for a bunch of cattle that were being driven through the country. Abe told him that he had seen a bunch of cattle that evening, so the next morning the marshal deputized Abe to go with them. Abe knew about where the men with their bunch of cattle would have had to camp the night before, so he rode almost straight to them. He said that when they got within sight of the cattle, the marshal took his six-shooter out of the holster on his belt, which was under his overcoat, placed it in his overcoat pocket, and left his hand in his pocket to hold the gun. As they got closer, Henry saw them and rode out to meet them. It was said of Henry that when he was riding horseback, he carried his gun slung across the pommel of his saddle rather than on his hip. Carried in this fashion, Henry could reach for his gun with lightning speed. He always thought of everything, apparently. Any sensible man knew that it was suicide to try to outdraw Henry, and apparently the marshal was no exception to the rule.

When they got within speaking distance, Henry asked Abe if he had brought those men over there. The marshal spoke up and said, "No, Henry, I brought Abe." Abe said that for a few minutes, Henry and the marshal both cussed each other out for all they were worth, and the marshal told Henry that he was going to look over the cattle. Henry replied that he wasn't. The marshal spoke to the boy who was helping Henry: "You ride on up ahead and hold up those cattle." Henry's voice cut in with a quiet deadliness. "Just don't you go anywhere! Stay right where you are." The boy waited and Henry turned loose another barrage of curses and innuendos against the marshal. After arguing for quite a while, Henry told the marshal that he and Abe could ride up to the front of the bunch, and one of them could come down on each side of the cattle and look at them, but they could not cut anything out or ride into the bunch. "If you ride into the bunch," Henry said, "you sure as hell might not come out again."

The two accepted the dictum. They rode down the herd, one on each side, and looked the cattle over. Abe said afterward that he saw cattle in the bunch that he knew the marshal was looking for, but when they got to the end, where Henry sat grim-faced, steely eyes warily watching, the marshal said to Abe in a voice that carried to Henry, "Abe, I guess there's nothing here that we want." Abe explained this by saying that the marshal had made the decision that to try to take them away from Henry would have been "too expensive!" Henry and his helper continued on their way, through the snow.

One more story about Henry's reactions to those who felt inclined to cross him, and then I will move on to another facet in Henry's many-sided nature. An old Spanish American man contributed this story. Henry had sold some cattle to two different buyers. One was purchasing cows from him, and the other was getting some yearlings. All the cattle were to be delivered at the same time by both buyers, at a point a couple of day's drive east of St. Johns, Arizona.

Henry's camp cook on the drive was a big young New Mexican of vast good nature, given to singing a lot and joking. He was a very good cook to boot. This young man was the kind who made a trail drive a pleasure to everyone. Almost any man who lived during the days when cattle were taken overland to the railroad shipping points will tell you that a good bunch of fellows in a drive made any trip enjoyable, while one or two misfits could spoil everything. Besides the cook, there were two other Anglos and several Spanish American cowboys. All were very congenial, and the trip went well. Henry himself was a good companion under such circumstances. He did his share of the work and liked to sit around the campfire at night, where among the circle of cowboys could be found something akin to perfection in the way of camaraderie. Henry would sometimes talk about his old friends and neighbors in Texas, when he was a boy, and about the country and the life he had led there. "What I can't understand," he would say, "is why in hell would people have a good country like that and come away out here to a sorry country like this?" He probably said it facetiously, but to be able to tell whether he was speaking with praise or censure about New Mexico and the life he had chosen so long ago, one would have had to be there—to sense the spoken words rather than to just read them.

Finally, the day arrived when the cattle reached the end of the journey. Now, as everyone knows who has sold cattle over the years, there are buyers, and then again there are buyers! Some are good, straight-shooting fellows who make all the details of the sale a pleasure. Then there are others: the fellows who cut back cattle on little or no pretext and who raise unforeseen objections. They are classed as the "tough buyers." There are some whom you have to worry about when the payoff is made. Will the check bounce, or will it be all right? Your entire income for the year is at stake. Checks were known to bounce after the ranchers' cattle were two states away by train. Perhaps their whole year of work and expense came to naught. Henry's two buyers might not have been the worst, but they had decided between themselves to put one over on Henry and make an unforeseen demand. Like many others before them, they underestimated their slender, mild-mannered seller. They told Henry that they wanted the cattle delivered directly to St. Johns, which would make another two days' drive for him and his crew. Little doubting that Henry would acquiesce, they delivered their ultimatum.

"We want them cattle in St. Johns," they told Henry.

"But that wasn't the agreement," Henry replied, an icy undertone edging its way into his voice. "You'll take them here, fellows, just like you said."

The buyers chose to remain cocky. "Oh no we won't," said one of them. "If you want your money, you'll take them on to St. Johns."

Henry suddenly became very quiet, but his wiry figure was tensed like a spring. Felipe Padilla, his long-time Quemado friend, moved to his side.[2] Both men wore guns, and their hands moved in a knowledgeable way near the holsters. This was almost a reflex with them. They may have had no ambitions to shoot anyone at all, but the two buyers weren't slow in appraising the situation. No one could fail to be aware of that inner hard core in the person of Henry Coleman—that certain glint of eye.

"Tell you what," said Henry, not raising his voice. "You pay my boys two days' extra wages, and you pay me too, and we'll take 'em on. And you'll pay for the extra chuck too. All expenses!" His voice was not loud but it was commanding, and then there was that very convincing big pearl-handled six-shooter on his hip, hanging way down low. The buyers agreed to everything quite readily. Arrangements were made, and the cattle and men headed toward the west.

When they got to St. Johns, they passed a nice big apple orchard on the edge of town, the rosy fruit hanging ripe and luscious on the trees. Since their fare along the way had been mostly beans, salt pork, biscuits, coffee, and occasionally beef, they were hungry for apples. Some of the men mentioned to Henry how good some fruit would taste. He agreed with them but said they must first ask permission from the man who owned the orchard. He would be willing to pay the owner for the fruit they ate, but first he had to ride on ahead and contact his buyers; the men could stay and eat their apples and he would pay the owner when he got back. As Henry rode off, the cowboys moved toward the house and orchard, mouths watering. A loud haloo, and another, and still another went unanswered. It did not take long for them to decide that under the circumstances the most sensible thing to do was to start eating.

The tree-ripened fruit tasted as good as it looked, and the men were happily picking and eating when the Mormon who owned the orchard rode up. His view of the affair was less than tolerant and he dressed them down in a fine rage. "Our boss will pay for them," they told him in chorus. "He said to go ahead and eat a few; he'll be right back and pay you."

"Oh, he did, did he?" the man waxed sarcastic. "Well, you were trespassing on my property and you're not going to get by with it." He paused a moment as though some thought has just occurred to him. "Who did you say your boss was?" he asked. When the answer came back, "Henry Coleman," the owner of the orchard seemed to be momentarily struck dumb. "Oh," he said in a calm tone. He turned away, saying as he went, "Go ahead boys, just eat all you want."

Notes

1. The monikers of "Salty John" and "Slash J. L." allegedly came from the legendary Ray Morley, for the two men who had the same name and who both lived in the Quemado area so the men would not be confused with one another. John William Cox Jr. was born at Mosheim, Bosque County, Texas, on August 3, 1851. In 1883 Cox and Noah McCustion drove a thousand head of cattle from Bosque County to the Datil and Mangas Mountains where Cox located his Slash J L Ranch. The ranch was located between Big Alegres and the Crosby and Mangas Mountains. The ranch headquarters was at the foot of Big Alegres; a nearby peak was named for Cox. On May 10, 1915, while Cox was hauling a wagonload of barbed wire to his ranch, a spool rolled off the wagon, caught his spur, and knocked him to the ground. The mules pulling the wagon were spooked and Cox was dragged to death. It was said at the time of his death that he had six thousand head of cattle and $250,000 in the bank. Tenth Census (1870) and 11th Census (1880), Bosque County, Texas; 14th Census (1910), Socorro County, NM; "John William Cox Jr. (1861–1915)," *Find A Grave*, accessed June 30, 2021, https://www.findagrave.com/memorial/43826968/john-william-cox.

   John "Salty John" Cox was born on February 15, 1874, in Mason County Texas. Cox's World War I draft card describes him as tall and slender with blue eyes and brown hair. For some unexplained reason, Cox often told people he was born in 1878 on his father's ranch on Agua Chiquita Creek near Weed, New Mexico. In June 1900, at the age of 26, after his widely publicized attempt to help Coleman escape from the Juárez jail, Cox married Sarah Dean Latham, and the couple took up ranching on Trujillo Creek in the foothills of the Black Range in Sierra County near Hillsboro. Three sons and a daughter were born to the couple. In Hillsboro Cox was involved in a feud and shouting match with the Sierra County sheriff, William C. "Billy" Kendall, which ended in Cox shooting and wounding Kendall. In 1910 Cox filed on 320 acres four miles east of Salt Lake. He later moved to Cow Springs near Salt Lake, where his oldest son, Robert, died at the age of 18.

In Magdalena in 1912, following his indictment for horse stealing, Cox
shot and killed Lige Carter. Cox blamed Carter, who was working on
the Nations Ranch at the time, for the indictment. Cox was arrested
by Deputy Sheriff Grant Milligan and was tried but acquitted when
he claimed that Carter had a knife and he feared for his life. John and
Sarah later divorced, and Sarah moved to Portland, Oregon, while John
remained on the Cow Springs ranch. Known for his tall tales, Cox later
remarried and moved to Albuquerque, where he died on July 14, 1954.
He was buried in Sunset Memorial Park. Cox told a WPA field writer,
N. Howard Thorp, a story about Henry Coleman that is not related in
the few biographical sketches of Coleman. According to this narrative,
Coleman, after escaping from jail in Ciudad Juárez, continued to sell
cattle around Silver City, Lake Valley, Las Cruces, and other towns that
"would drift" into the United States from Mexico. One day Coleman,
accompanied by one of his men, went into Silver City to cash some
checks and ran into four men from whom he had stolen cattle. When
the men, all of whom were mounted, accused Coleman of stealing their
cattle, a gun battle erupted in which Coleman killed two of the men and
wounded two others, and rode out of town. Afterward, Coleman confined
himself to the theft of cattle from Mexico. Later, in the Quemado area,
both men, perhaps rustling from one another, came to despise the other.
Eleventh Census (1880), Mason County, TX; 13th Census (1900) and
14th Census (1910), Sierra County, NM; 14th Census (1920), Socorro
County, NM; 15th Census (1930) and 16th Census (1940), Catron
County, NM; 16th Census (1940), Multnomah County, Oregon; John
T. Cox World War I Draft Card, ancestry.com; *Albuquerque Journal*,
April 9, 1912; N. Howard Thorp, "Henry Coleman" interview, *New
Mexico Archives Online*, accessed July 23, 2021, https://nmarchives.
unm.edu/repositories/10/archival_objects/18383. The original copy of
Thorp's interview with "Long John" is at the New Mexico State
Records Center and Archives in Santa Fe. For an interesting interview
with Cox in 1953, see "John 'Salty John' Cox: Handy with a Gun and
His Fists," in Bryan, *True Tales of the American Southwest*, 93–107.
For a sanitized biographical sketch of Cox, see *Fence Lake, New
Mexico Area: Families & History* (Fence Lake, NM: Fence Lake Book
Committee, 1985), 55.

2. Various censuses list Felipe Padilla as born in 1865, 1867, or 1869.
The oldest of six sons born to Francisco Padilla and Josefa Sanchez,
Padilla spent his early life at Mangas, where he never attended school

but worked with sheep and then with cattle. He later married Sofia, twenty-two years his junior, and the two raised six sons and two daughters. In 1940, at the age of 75, Padilla was living at Prairie View, west of Quemado, with his wife and daughter Ana Maria, and still working as a cattleman. Along with Coleman, Ed Oliver, and Hugh Neighbor, Padilla was charged with the murder of Frank Bourbonnaise in 1919 but acquitted. Fourteenth Census (1910) and 15th Census (1920), Socorro County, NM; 16th Census (1930) and 17th Census (1940), Catron County, NM.

Chapter 7

Clara Coleman

T here is another facet that helps explain what made Henry Coleman tick. This is something on which all who knew him seemed to be agreed: Henry was quite a "ladies' man." And why wouldn't he be? He was handsome and suave; he rode good horses, he dressed well, and he cut a gallant figure wherever he went. Women were charmed by him. He also had the added attraction of being rather mysterious.

He seems to have had various female friends around the country, and hard feelings understandably developed between him and his swarthy helpmate, Clara. After a few years together in the Quemado country, he and Clara separated, and Clara got a place farther up Largo Canyon than where their first home was. She received the place, one hundred head of cattle, and some of the best horses that she and Henry had acquired.

One elderly lady gave me a good description of Clara Coleman's appearance. "She was slender and mannish," she said. "Very dark. Undoubtedly, she had Indian blood. She always wore pants and an old flop hat. I don't know if she ever had a dress to her name. She worked like a man, rode, built fence, and did just about anything. She was a good-hearted woman. I believe she would have given anyone who needed it her last dime."

Just across Largo Creek to the east from where Clara lived, there was a family named Bourbonnaise (pronounced "Boor-bun-ay"). At one time Clara was very friendly with the Bourbonnaises, but later they had trouble.[1]

Down the creek from Clara, there was another neighbor, O. D. Collins.[2] Collins ran sheep on the Largo and he had a little hotel in town, which is where he usually stayed when in Quemado. In later years I met Collins, who drove back to the Quemado country to look over his old haunts, and he told me one very revealing story about Clara Coleman. One summer, he said, there was a bad drought, and his part of the creek dried up completely, so that he had no water for his sheep. Farther up the Largo, Clara still had plenty of water, but there were some cross fences there to divide off people's access to the water, and he had none. He was half afraid to approach Clara about the possibility of using her part of the creek, because he had heard she was a pretty tough character, but finally in desperation he went to her and asked her if he could water his sheep on her part of the creek. "My water!" she exclaimed. "That isn't my water. Mr. Collins, it's the Lord's. He put it there for all of us. Of course, you can use it."[3]

There is no doubt that Clara, like her husband, was an enigma— a curious mixture of contradictory qualities. She had aided and abetted Henry in his early rustling years on the Largo, and doubtlessly she knew all about him. It was Clara who had whisked the Indians' cattle out of the corral at the Record place. She showed the same enigmatic pattern of good and bad as Henry. She doubtless had her troubles, and some of these proved to be other women who were attracted to Henry. Not a glamorous type, she sought apparently to justify her lack of pulchritude by working hard. She drove a team of small mules and made trips to Quemado in her wagon. Clara and her little mules were a familiar sight in the small community. A Spanish American cowboy worked for her after she and Henry separated, and she hired another

young man by the name of Don Oliver.[4] Don was only about 20 years old, while Clara was in her 50s.

It is a sad fact that in any rural community, scandal is the succulent dish that is personally stewed by every person who possesses a certain type of imagination plus a loose tongue. It does not have to be bolstered necessarily by facts; a little whispered gossip can set it flourishing most healthily. Gossip had it, of course, that Clara Coleman was cohabiting with her young employee, albeit he was young enough to be her son. For reasons best known to himself, Henry apparently fanned the flame of this rumor. I have heard this explained by at least one person who said that Henry though that if he could get this rumor circulating as a full-fledged scandal, it might turn some sentiment in his favor.

Such a situation was denied by the Spanish American man who worked for Clara. "We had our own room in that house, Don [Oliver] and me," he said. "My wife was in Quemado and Don didn't have a wife. We both ran some cattle on her place, in return for the work

we did for her." Still another voice dissents with the long-buried scandalous gossip. This is the voice of a woman, then a teenager, who was Don Oliver's girlfriend. She taught school, and she and Don hoped to get married. "Don's folks were short on grass," she told me. "He made a deal with Clara Coleman to pasture some of his cattle on her place, and to work and help her in return." She told me that Don petulantly told her that he hated the deal. "Now I've got to work for that old woman!" he said. This young woman had her own versions of Henry Coleman. To her he was one to strike terror into the hearts of all young females. "My stepdad knew him well in Texas," she said. "They went to school together and my stepdad said he was always a mean devil. I was always just scared to death of him. One time I went to a dance at a ranch house out north of town.

"In those days, people often gave dances at their homes, and we'd dance until sunup. Henry showed up at that dance. He was courting other women around the country and one of the women was there that night. A nephew of this woman's husband came to me and asked me, 'Can you keep your mouth shut?'" K. evidently told him she could, so he led her to a window, just outside of which Henry was talking to his ladylove. She then found herself standing between the nephew and the lovers, and was so scared that she said afterward she could not remember a word that was said. I asked her why the nephew wanted her to hear what was said, rather than just to hear it himself. "I think," she replied, "that his idea was to try to find out whether or not Henry and her might have been hatching up some scheme to do away with his uncle, and he wanted to have a witness to it."

This scary opinion of Henry was apparently not shared by an elderly lady who ran a small boarding house in early-day Quemado, and whom we shall call Mrs. L.[5] She saw enough in her day to fill a dozen books, and she had an outgoing way about her that won her many friends. She was a fine cook, and her dining room attracted many of those old-time cowboys and ranchers, who made her little place of business their headquarters. Young schoolmarms found Mrs. L.'s hotel a pretty fair marriage mart; they would board with Mrs. L. and soon would know all the eligible bachelors in the country, and unless they were so homely that they had to slip up on the dipper to drink at night, they would not stay single long! Over cups of Mrs. L.'s good boiled coffee, the men of the country met, swapped tales, made deals, and traded. Of Henry, who stopped there often, she said, "We enjoyed his company. He was always a gentleman. He would give my little girl a fifty-cent piece nearly every time he came by and she would go and sit on his lap. Often, he brought presents—a little live cottontail rabbit, or a chipmunk, or some candy. He always sat with his back against the wall; never near any window. He was a quiet man, not much given to joshing or joking."

Notes

1. According to the family Bible, Aaron F. Bourbonnaise was born on April 11, 1863, during the Civil War frontier violence, into a large Quaker family in Kansas. He was the son of Mary Ann Anderson and Antoine (Anthony) A. S. Bourbonnaise, a Pottawatomie Indian, who had

been married at Silver Lake in Jackson County, Kansas, in June 1856. When the Pottawatomies were expelled from Kansas Territory, the family moved to a reserve in Indian Territory. On June 8, 1886, Aaron Bourbonnaise was married to Caliste A. Crapper in the Chickasaw Nation. In 1891 Aaron Bourbonnaise was working for the Indian Police at the Sac and Fox Agency. The father, Antoine Bourbonnaise, died at Shawneetown in December 1891. By 1900 Aaron was working as a farmer near Clarendon, Ochiltree County, Texas. One son, Arthur Levi, was born in 1891, followed by four daughters: Isabelle in 1893, Mary Ozetta in 1897, Lola in 1899, and Aurelia in 1902, all named after family members. Aaron eventually moved the family, along with his aging mother, back to what had become the state of Oklahoma, where his wife, Caliste, died. In 1907 Aaron is listed in the *City Directory* at Shawnee, where he had acquired a small piece of property, as a laborer. By 1916 the family was still in Oklahoma. There Mary Ozetta Bourbonnaise enlisted in the US Army in the last months of World War I. The burial site of Aaron F. Bourbonnaise has not been located. In the 1922 Indian census in Oklahoma. thirty-one individuals with the name Bourbonnaise, including three persons named Frank Bourbonnaise, are all enumerated. Besides their Oklahoma, Texas, and New Mexico history, the family had close Minnesota connections, and when Lola was subpoenaed to testify in Socorro, her registered mail receipt was returned from Waubun, Mahnomen County, Minnesota, where there was a small Pottawatomie reservation and where the family may have fled after Coleman killed Aaron. Shortly after the family left New Mexico, the matriarch of the family, Mary Ann, died in 1921. Isabelle met and married a French Canadian, Joseph Napoleon Guyon (not to be confused with the famous professional football player), at Quemado, New Mexico, where a son was born in 1917. A daughter, Geraldine Lola, was born in Minnesota two years later. Lola Guyon died at age 27 in Oklahoma and was buried at the Tecumseh Mission in Pottawatomie County. Her husband, who later remarried, coached baseball at Clemson University. The Guyon son, Joseph Francis, taught high school at Quemado in 1940. Lola married a man named Thompson and died on the Pottawatomie Reserve in Oklahoma on July 30, 1928. Aurelia married a Henry J. Thompson at Clay, Minnesota, in June 1924, and two daughters were born there. She remarried in October 1930 in Noble, Oklahoma, this time to an oil driller named John J. Capes. She lived until August 1998, dying in rural

Texas near Beeville. Ozette (Ozetta) married a man named Harry M. Bylesby in Oklahoma in November 1926. She died at the age of 97 in Clearwater, Florida, in December 1994. *Christian Worker* 24 (January–July 1894), *1907 Shawnee City Directory*, and US Indian Census, 1891, 1892, 1895, 1900, and 1930, all on ancestry.com, accessed July 19, 2021; 13th Census (1900), Ochiltree County, TX; 14th Census (1910), Pottawatomie County, OK; 15th Census (1920), Mahnomen County, MN; *Victoria* (TX) *Advocate,* October 1, 1998; *Corpus Christi Caller,* October 1, 1998; *Tampa Bay Times*, December 13, 1994.

2. Othello D. Collins, who signed his name "Ody," was known in the Quemado area as O. D. He was born on August 28, 1884, in McClellan County, Texas, and is described on his World War I draft card as tall, with blue eyes and light hair. In February 1909 Collins wed Lola McCabe, and the couple raised two daughters and a son. At age 25 Collins was running a sheep ranch at Sterling City, Texas, northwest of San Angelo, where a younger brother joined him, along with three Mexican-born sheepherders. By 1920 he and his wife had moved to Quemado, where he ran a small hotel while maintaining a small sheep ranch. Returning to Texas, Collins died at San Angelo on January 27, 1971, and was buried at Sterling City. Thirteenth Census (1900), Johnson County, TX; 14th Census (1910), Sterling County, TX; 15th Census (1920), Socorro County, NM; "Othello D. Collins," Ancestry.com, https://www.ancestry.com/discoveryui-content/view/28902269:60525; Texas Death Certificate, Ancestry.com; Social Security Application and Claims Index, US Social Security Applications and Claims Index, 1936–2007, Ancestry. com; Texas County Marriage Records, Texas, US, County Marriage Records, 1817–1965, Ancestry.com.

3. Langford Johnston, who was working for the Slash JL Ranch north of the Datil Mountains, recalled how in 1917 two horses that had been purchased from Henry Coleman were lost, and he was sent to retrieve the animals, who were thought to have strayed back to the Coleman homestead on Largo Creek north of Quemado. Johnston arrived at the homestead late in the afternoon and watched as Clara Coleman came riding up. Clara said the horses were in a canyon five miles away. Not only did Clara feed his horse, but she also fed Johnston with biscuits, gravy, and a large steak, put him up for the evening, and rode with him the next morning to where the horses were grazing. Langford Ryan Johnston, *Old Magdalena, Cow Town* (Albuquerque: Cottonwood Printing, 1983), 21–22.

4. Donovan Mackey Oliver was born at Mineral Wells in Palo Pinto County, Texas, on July 17, 1898, the youngest son of Mattie Aldridge and Edward Dionysius Oliver on July 17, 1898. His parents had been married in Bastrop, Texas, on Christmas Day 1877. Shortly before his death he was described as tall, with blue eyes and light-colored hair. At one time or another, all of his brothers—Roy Scott, Edward Dionysius Jr., and Cap Hill—worked selling dry goods. Listing his occupation as that of a well driller, he moved to Quemado shortly after the death of his father, Edward Dionysius Oliver, with his mother, Mattie Aldridge (or Aldrich) Oliver, when Clara Coleman employed him as a hired hand. He was only 20 when he was murdered at the Coleman Ranch on December 11, 1918. He was buried in the Magdalena Community Cemetery. His mother moved back to Texas and passed away on September 21, 1926, at the age of 67, in Mineral Wells; she was buried beside her husband in Dallas. Thirteenth Census (1900) and 14th Census (1910), Palo Pinto County, TX; *Find a Grave*, accessed February 27, 2021, www.lbjf.org/aud/tel-wh/187903-aud-tel-wh-06155.mp3; World War I Draft Card, Ancestry.com; Texas, US, Death Certificates, 1903–1982, Ancestry.com, accessed March 21, 2021.

5. This hotel was owned by Kentucky-born Fannie Graham, age 37, the wife of James A. Graham, a mechanic. The Grahams later ran the post office in Datil for several years. A second hotel in Quemado was owned by Texas-born Lola B. Collins and her husband, O. D. Collins. Fifteenth Census (1920), Socorro County, NM; Jim Wagner, *Datil: A Hidden History of an Historic New Mexico Town* (self-published, 2022), 19–32.

Chapter 8

Trust in a Lawless Land

U nderneath the average façade of being fashionably uncurious, every man wonders avidly about every other man. The man who buys a little paperback novel and sticks it in his pocket to take home thinks to find in its pages something that will complement his own life, his own experiences, or his own longings. Because of the fact that we all are constantly measuring our own experiences by the yardstick of what we know of the experiences of other, we may ponder, then, on what kind of a romantic Henry Coleman might really have been. The movies and TV never—well, almost never—divorce high adventure from high romance. Was Henry the lover in the best Hollywood style, or did he banter lightly with his women and never let them really know what was in his mind or his heart? Did he relegate them to that dull stall in the barn, labeled as being from the "fair sex"? And from which stall she is led out from time to time, to be paraded as a "lady," but never as an individual? The inhabitants of the "fair sex" stall are nicely groomed and well fed, but they are never wondered about as an equal spirit. And they are inside the stall more than they are out of it.

Did Henry think about women in general as the "fair sex," defer to them as such, take off his hat to them when he met them on the street, and secretly despise them? Or did he think of them merely as practicable fixtures to have around? One might suspect the latter attitude in Clara's case. She was not pretty, she was older than Henry, she was an indefatigable worker, and she may well have done lots of chores that Henry preferred not to worry about. There we have all the ingredients of an unromantic situation! It must be assumed that Henry was not particularly faithful to Clara, and that in time she knew about his infidelity and finally took steps to justify her own pride as a woman.

But then we wonder if there was a woman in Henry's life who really called the turns, who ruled his thoughts and his heart, and who might have transformed him into the knightly hero who is supposed, by rights, to dwell within any being so dashing and as bold and as charismatic a character as was Henry Coleman. Perhaps, but in real life there is no director to guarantee that the leading man will come on stage at the opportune moment, if at all. Henry doubtlessly caused more than his share of feminine hearts to flutter, but the wheels of his mind were perhaps geared to running too adroitly to allow any incautious profusions of sentiment, or for any highly romantic stances where the heart is unwarily worn on the sleeve or the banner of love waved for all to see. He tended, probably, to hide his true emotions when he saw the unmistakable signs of a woman about to throw all caution to the winds and fall head over heels in love with him. Henry probably saw to it that he should profit from such a happy situation, but from the clues we have of his nature, no woman ever knew all about Henry Coleman. The most accurate concept we might have of Henry, in regards to women, is of a man charming but restrained, confident of his manly appeal but withholding the core of his being from any mere woman.

Perhaps the nearest that Henry ever came to being relaxed were the times when he brought baby rabbits to the little girl in the hotel. In such an act, some very simple part of his nature came out of hiding and walked in the sun. But on the whole, Henry was not a simple man in any sense of the word.

Mrs. L.'s particular friends did not bother with the formality of sitting in the regular dining room. They liked to go in the back door to the kitchen, sit and sip coffee, and visit with her as she went about her work. At mealtime she served her food family style, waiting on her customers with grace and goodwill. Henry liked the informality of the kitchen sippers, and on one particular day, he was sitting in the kitchen, draped companionably over a cup of coffee, and exchanging friendly banter with his hostess. In the front room where meals were served, several men had already gathered. The front door slammed, and the loud voice of one of Henry's worst enemies could be heard. He had an unmistakable way of talking; no one could be in doubt about who he was.

The good lady shook in her shoes. She shot an oblique look at Henry, but his expression never changed; the hand that held the coffee cup traveled with steady precision from table to mouth and back to the table. Not a word was said. The loud monologue drifted in to them from the front room, blustering talk interspersed with plenty of cussing. "Oh dear!" she thought to herself. "And they've been packing guns for each other for a long time now!" In a state of panic, she circled the situation in her mind, wondering if there was anything she could do. "I'll ask George D.," she finally decided. "He'll tell me what to do." George was in the front room, but when Mrs. L. streaked through the room and gave him a furtive beckon, he followed her out the front door. She led him around the corner of the building, then turned and clutched his arm, her eyes wide with alarm. "George, what shall I do?" she beseeched him. "You know who just came in, and Henry's back there in the kitchen, drinking coffee. They'll kill each other! Right here in my house, there'll be a killing. What should I do?"

He smiled. "No need to be afraid," he told her. "There ain't neither one of them boys goin' to do a thing in your home. They have that much respect for you; won't neither one do nothin'. You don't worry now!" He patted her arm.

She hurried back to her kitchen, still scared. Even as she went through the front room, the men who were going to eat with her that day were taking their places at the tables. Henry Coleman was walking slowly into the dining room, a study in expressionless unconcern. His enemy was still holding forth in his usual loud tones. Henry took his place at the table. The monologue never slowed down. Both men sat there, never even glancing at each other. They both ate heartily. The loud one kept up a steady stream of chatter. Henry said nothing. The meal was finally over, and both men walked their separate ways. All was peaceful. The gallantry of the day and time was equally shared by two men—one of the smooth and impeccable manners, when he chose, and the other the rough-talking one of no particular manners. Yet both gentlemen, according to their day.

Mrs. L. had some little experience to tell me about Ben Foster, Henry's factotum and troubleshooter. She described him as a rough-looking character, with none of Henry's likable ways or polish. He kept a room at her little hotel, where he stayed when he was in the country. It was taken for granted that that was Ben's room. He came and went, and his room was held for him.

One night Mrs. L. thought she heard Ben come in, in the wee small hours, and go into his room. When daylight came, Ben did not appear on the scene, and Mrs. L. wondered whether she had really heard him or had dreamed that she had. As the hours wore by and no sound came from his room, Mrs. L. got curious. She decided that she would peek into the room and see if there was anyone inside. She tiptoed to the door, and very gently, very slowly turned the knob. The knob squeaked faintly as she turned it. Very slowly she pushed on the door, opening it just a crack. The next thing she did was let out an abrupt scream. She was looking directly into the barrel end of two big six-shooters. Ben fortunately was not trigger happy; he preferred to see who he was shooting at, but there he sat, a gun in each hand.

As it quickly registered on his mind who his prying acquaintance was, he spoke, somewhat shakily.

"Mrs. L.," he said sternly, "don't you never do that again! I wouldn't harm you for the world, let alone kill you. Now don't never do that no more!" She didn't.

The depredations on cattle and horses continued as long as Henry was in the country. Everyone knew, or at least surmised, that Henry had his helpers—individuals who performed their given jobs, for a price, were responsible. But apparently there were some who occasionally felt that they were not paid enough to cover the risks they ran.

One of these was a little man known as Shorty, who had worked a long time on a ranch near Fox Mountain. During an interval when he was not working for his regular employer, he came driving through Quemado one day, headed south, in a light wagon drawn by two teams—two fine-looking mules and two equally good-looking horses. He had apparently come a long way, perhaps from Gallup. From what Mrs. L. could learn, he was headed for Mexico. This was a job he had been hired to do, and he had been given a little money in advance, and then he had collected some money at the northern end of his trip, perhaps from something that he had taken to Gallup and sold. Ben Foster knew about the whole transaction, and Shorty was supposed to hand over the money, or part of it, to his "bosses." He had other ideas.

Stopping over in Quemado to sleep, eat, and rest his teams, he called Mrs. L. aside and gave her his money to keep for him. In those days there was this surprising element of trust in a lawless land. Perhaps it can best be explained by the fact that a man has to trust someone. It is, and was then, a basic human need, demanding fulfillment as much as the stomach demands to be fed. Today we have our mechanized forms of trust: banks, with their rules and regulations; savings bonds; savings and loan companies; and all the regimented lines of business that handle men's funds for a fee. In those days people depended upon each other, and there existed an etiquette of the trust bestowed upon one man by another, which was perhaps just as invincible as the laws that govern banks today. The first thing involved was "Who to trust?" Men knew; they had an instinct for it. Shorty knew; perhaps many men who stopped with this gracious lady knew that she was trustworthy. She had been a banker for many of them. If there were occasional characters who might have raided her depository, there were more who would have defended her and rendered such an incident impossible. Mrs. L. knew, too, whom she could depend on. She took Shorty's money and put it deep down in a sturdy old trunk that she always kept locked.

In due time Ben approached Shorty for the money, and Shorty intimated that he no longer had it—that he had earned it and had left it with a friend for safekeeping. Ben must have satisfied himself that Shorty did not have the money on his person; he either knew or suspected that Mrs. L. was Shorty's banker, and the situation became tense. Ben was tough and surly by nature, and Mrs. L. was frankly worried. Would Ben try to take the money away from her? Would he demand it?

Soon he came to her and asked her if she had it. Yes, she said, she did. He explained to her that the money was to be turned over to Henry, and he asked her for it. Few men, and fewer women, could have been anything but apprehensive when confronted by a man like Ben Foster, demanding something they had and he claimed! But Mrs. L. was a brave woman, and she defended the trust that had been placed in her.

"I have it," she told Ben. "But Shorty gave it to me to keep for him. I promised him I would." Ben glowered at her and left.

Mrs. L. admitted that this made her very nervous. Would Ben come back and actually try to take it away from her? He was in an ugly mood. She watched as Ben rode off on horseback, headed up the Largo toward the old Estes place, where he had been staying.

Shorty came back later and contacted her, got his money, and left in the direction of Fox Mountain. Mrs. L. decided to ask for the help and the advice of a trusted Spanish American friend, another man whom people did not fool with. She confided in him and told him what had taken place. Placido reassured her. He would ride up and talk to Ben, he said, and she need not fear. It was six or seven miles up to the Estes place, and Placido rode the distance to ease his friend's mind, and to satisfy himself that she had nothing to worry about. He found Ben and told him that he must not bother Mrs. L. further about this money.[1] Mrs. L. heard no more from Ben about the matter. If there is one moral to be drawn from this episode, there might be several. Not only is the heart lifted by the flawlessness of trust but also by the knowledge that in those days, a man thought nothing of jogging a round trip of fourteen miles or so, on a horse, to put a friend's mind at ease. It might be difficult to achieve a favor of this dimension over the telephone today.

Note

1. Robert E. Lee Estes was born at Pennington, Trinity County, Texas, on January 6, 1865. By 1920 he had moved to Quemado and acquired a ranch near Salt Lake, where he was assisted by his sons, Sealy, Richard, and Albert. Seely Cosby Estes was on the Salt Lake Ranch for twelve years when he volunteered for the army at age 31 in May 1918 and was assigned to the 62nd Infantry; he died of the Spanish flu at Camp Fremont, near Palo Alto, California, on land leased from Stanford University, on October 20, 1918, and was buried in Magdalena. By 1930 R. E. L. Lewis had moved with his wife, Emily, to Buckhorn in Grant County, where he was working as a laborer on a farm at the age of 65 and living in a rented house valued at ten dollars; he was near his son, Albert, who had purchased a farm at nearby Gila. After a short stay at Clifton, Arizona, R. E. L. Estes later moved to Magdalena and died at the age of 76 on January 30, 1941. 1870 Census, Trinity County, TX; 1920 Census, Socorro County, NM; 1930 Census, Grant County, NM; Richard A. Estes, Sealey Estes, and Albert C. Estes World War I draft registration cards at US World War I Draft Registration Cards, 1917–1918, Ancestry.com; New Mexico World War I Records, 1917–1919, Ancestry.com.

Chapter 9

Murders on the Largo

B y this time in Henry Coleman's life, the dust was stirred up by so many unscrupulous activities it began to gather in big miasmic clouds. Rumblings were heard on the horizons of Henry's existence. In puzzlement we can turn again to the contradictory testimony of friend and foe. I view those words, uttered with such conviction, and try to examine them for what they are worth, and for what light they can shed on the checkered career of one very complex individual.

One man said feelingly, "Everything bad you heard about Coleman was probably true. He had a mean streak." Another old-timer of flawless character and reputation said just as convincingly, "I knew him well and liked him. Oh, of course, I didn't admire some of the things he did, but I'll say one thing. I never did catch him in a lie—not to me!" He reminisced further.

One time I had to go up the Largo to assess the value of his cattle and his place, for a finance company. I found everything just like Henry said it was. We were both on horseback and at one point, we turned around and saw a man on horseback trailing us. He was an individual we both knew, and he sure wasn't any friend of Henry's either. Well, Henry turned and rode back toward him and told him right out that there wasn't room enough on that side of the canyon for both of them, and to get going. The fellow left. I think he wanted to know just what Henry had up there, and thought he'd look over Henry's spread from a safe distance, while I am counting his cattle.

Another night, I had to go see Henry about something and I got there after dark in my Model T Ford. I drove right up to the door. Mrs. Coleman answered my call. Right behind her stood Henry, holding a .30-30 rifle. He yelled out. "Come right in, Jim! I didn't know who you were!"

In the Deed Record Book No. 90 in the old Socorro County records is a warrant deed, executed on April 16, 1917, and made from Henry Coleman to Clara Coleman. This deed described part of the ranch on the Largo, which was owned by Clara from that time until the day of her death. Henry deeded another piece of land—the rest of the Largo place—to Clara on February 11, 1918.

An old abstract shows how Henry got this land. On August 14 and 15, respectively, of 1916, two adjoining pieces of property were sold to Henry Coleman by Edward C. Wade and Alice Casey Hunt, and Charles Hunt, her husband.[1] In January of 1917, another piece of deeded land was conveyed to Henry by the Farr Sheep Co.[2] All of this deeded land together came to about 440 acres. That was not much land in terms of what land in this part of New Mexico would take care of in the way of cattle and horses, but it controlled the precious waters of the Largo, and the range to the east and west of it was all open. This was the place, then, that Henry settled and where he and Clara came to the parting of their ways.

In January of 1918, Clara Coleman deeded an undivided interest in forty acres of some of her deeded land to one Oran Wilkes.[3] Then three months later, on March 18, 1918, Clara was granted a divorce from Henry, after she sued on the grounds of abandonment.

The place that Clara Coleman was given when she separated from Henry was situated on the Largo Creek. Droughts through the 1930s, '40s and '50s depleted the springs that fed this once-fine source of water, but in those days, a big stream of clear water ran past her door, just a short distance east of the house. The house itself had been built specifically for Clara on the west bank of the Largo by E. E. Engle of Quemado.[4] It was built in the form of a square, out of hand-hewn pine logs. In the parlor of the four-room dwelling, the southeast room, there was a large, open fireplace. The chimney was unique in that it had, altogether, three separate fireplaces, all using the same flue. Smaller fireplaces with the same chimney heated the two bedrooms, which were the northeast and northwest rooms of the structure. Subsequent owners took down the house logs and moved them to another location, but the old three-fireplace chimney still stands today. Floodwaters that ran down an old water lane, which came into the Largo Creek from the west, have washed in mud and silt to a height of about three feet, covering the fireplaces themselves.

While Clara Coleman was waiting for her house to be finished, she lived in a small rock dugout west of the house, which had been built by a homesteader.[5] Her days in that abode were bound to be most primitive. Later, she used the dugout for a cellar.

There was an old hand-dug well in the yard, just east of the house, that supplied water for home use. A huge cottonwood tree spread its great limbs protectively over the house itself—the biggest tree of its kind along the creek. Actually, the house was set quite far back from the creek, and between it and the running water was a large grove of beautiful trees—mountain cottonwoods as they are called, which trace the course of the Largo for miles with their cool, emerald greenery. After a rain the cottonwood groves exude a delicious odor, like ripe apples. In dry, drought years, the line of cottonwoods along the creek are sometimes the only green growing thing around, and they do their part to keep up appearances. Dappled shadows play over the ground beneath them, and deer step tentatively in their protective shade. The wind calls forth a variety of rushing music from their leafy branches: shrill tunes in the leafless winter months and soft billowing lullabies in the summer. Behind the house to the west was the shed-like barn and a large corral, flanked by hills, which held the secrets of prehistoric ruins. These hills were, and remain, covered with ancient crumbled pueblos of Indians who lived in great numbers along the Largo at least eight hundred years ago, or longer, but who were gone from the scene when the Spanish conquistadores made their earliest forays into what is now New Mexico. It is said that Clara, with characteristic energy, liked to explore these ruins, and that she spent a good deal of time digging in them and recovered many interesting artifacts.

It is hard to imagine how she found time for anything of that sort; just the business of living took so much time and energy, and Clara always had her shoulder to the wheel when there was any work to be done, whether it was cooking, building fence, or taking care of the cattle. South and east of Clara's home on the Largo, the ten-thousand-foot-high Escondido Mountain rose in solitary splendor, the only real mountain anywhere near.[6] It treated Clara and all the dwellers in the valley to its colorful moods, just as it had shared them with human inhabitants for hundreds of years; white with a blue-coated army of trees swarming its slopes in the winter, its crest blazing with yellow in autumn as the quaking aspen relinquish their summer green, and glowing a rosy plum color on a summer evening, just at sunset, the dying crimsons accentuated by bright yellow cliffs, the blue and purple deep of the hills falling away from the yellows. Lower hills and mesas lying east and west of the creek were covered by scrubby growths of piñons and cedar. It was, and still is, a good cow country, offering much protection with its hills and trees and with a good deal of browse—more then than now. In this beautiful setting, Clara pursued her way of life with her land, her cattle, and her string of saddle horses. She may or may not have been aware of the dark fate that was approaching, which has never been solved to anyone's satisfaction.

To the east of her home, and only one-quarter of a mile away, lived the Bourbonnaise family. True to form, the stories come to us in full conflict. "Bourbonnaise was a fine man, a peaceable fellow." "Bourbonnaise was a mean son of a gun, a troublemaker, a source of potential danger to Clara, with whom it is proved that he did fall out."

The stories jump and dance to the different tunes! Perhaps the best straight account of the facts came from the Spanish American man who worked for Clara Coleman in 1916, and whose coworker was young Don Oliver.

Clara Coleman, as stated before, had one hundred head of cattle, which she had acquired in a separate agreement with Henry. She had also made arrangements to obtain two hundred more head, some of them from a neighbor, Epifanio Baca.[7] He delivered all but twelve of these cattle. During the first part of December, he finally got the remaining twelve head together, and on the morning of December 12, he arrived at Clara's ranch with the small herd. He was accompanied by another Spanish American who was helping him drive the cattle. They put the cattle in the big corral, just west of the Coleman house, and waited for quite a while, thinking that someone would come out. Their arrival had been well advertised by their whooping and yelling as they drove the cattle into the corral. When no one appeared, they started to the house. There was a light sprinkling of snow on the ground, and when they reached the little porch on the east side of the house, Epifanio leaned down and started to take off his spurs. At this point his helper yelled out. Epifanio stopped fumbling with the spur straps and looked to see what his friend found so surprising. The man was pointing to fresh dog tracks outside the house. The tracks were bloody, and the dog had been going in and out through the outside door, which the men noticed was open. Epifanio forgot about his spurs, and both men hurried to the door and looked in. The younger man, who was ahead, let out a scream. "They're dead!" he cried. "There's someone dead in there!" Epifanio ran in, and there on the floor lay the stiff and lifeless bodies of Clara Coleman and Don Oliver. They had been killed hours earlier and there was blood everywhere. Both had been shot and both bodies had toppled partly into the big, open fireplace as they fell and both were burned to some degree. Don Oliver's hand was badly burned, and Clara's face and hair were burned.

Apparently, Don Oliver had been sitting by the fire with his bedroom slippers on. It was thought that he was shot first and that

Clara was shot as she came rushing in to see what was happening. In reconstructing the scene, it was suggested that it would be easier to shoot a woman, therefore the murderer probably shot the young man first.

Oliver's fellow worker, the Spanish American cowboy, had gone to Quemado the day before. "I would have been keeled myself," he said, "because I was running some cattle up there and was working to pay out by pasture bill. That is what Don Oliver was doing too. He brought some heifers over there. But my wife, he [*sic*] was seeck—about to have a baby—so I go home to stay with heem, and not been there. Eef I ben there, I would been keeled, like Oliver."

There were two distinct schools of thought about who did the killings: those disposed to think that Clara had been killed by Ben Foster, hired at the behest of Henry to liquidate her, and those who thought that Frank Bourbonnaise, helped by a friend or perhaps by several friends, had done the killings. Clara's helper who had escaped with his life because his wife was about to "produce" favored the latter theory. Bourbonnaise had been trying to buy her place from her, he said, and had gotten pretty nasty when she refused to sell. Furthermore, big calves of hers kept disappearing; the cows would show up with tight bags, and on one or two occasions, they found where someone had brazenly cut her fence and driven the prospective beef through to be butchered. This deed was done within a stone's throw of her home, as though the butcher or butchers might be taunting her. Clara and her friends figured that Bourbonnaise was doing the butchering.

Nor was the fence cutting limited to one faction. When Bourbonnaise came to the country and settled in the house just across the creek from Clara, he fenced off a pasture for himself, through which came trails to water, the trails used by Clara's cattle. With her strongly entrenched ideas about divine water rights, this to Clara was criminal. Doubtlessly, she tried to reason with Bourbonnaise, but when negotiations failed, Clara resorted to more high-handed solutions. She cut the fences where the trails went through. In fact, the entire history of the western frontier abounds with killings over fence lines and water holes.

The Spanish American cowboy had warned Clara about Bourbonnaise. "That fellow, he keel you!" he had told her. She always laughed it off, saying that she had several guns in her possession and knew how to use them. "Yes," said her helper, "but when we ride, we go different ways, me, one way, you another, Don Oliver another. Bourbonnaise could get you while you are alone." But Clara was too tough to listen, and she was not afraid.

The killing had been cannily planned. It was probably snowing as the killer, or killers, crept up outside the house, and it was already dark. The sound of the storm nullified any noise they might have made, and the snow quickly covered all their tracks.

One other hapless witness had heard all the commotion in the night. A sheepherder from Childers' place, ten miles up the Largo from the Coleman house, had left his camp that day to ride to Quemado.[8] He rode in the traditional sheepherder manner, sitting well back on the rump of his little burro, and when darkness started to fall, he stopped for the night on a small hill just west and south of the Coleman house, above the corral. He was awakened in the night by the sound of several shots. Shivering in his blankets the rest of the night, he could hardly have been human if he had gone back to sleep. People were quite courageous in those days, but to be alone in the night and to know that killers are close by hardly adds to a feeling of personal safety. He could not have afforded to build a fire, so he just had to sweat it out until daylight alone and in the dark. In the morning he hastened to town to report what he had heard, but before he had a chance to relate his tale, Epifanio Baca and his cowboy had discovered the full extent of the crime.

One of Clara's neighbors had seen and heard a few things in town; namely, some men had been drinking together, and one of them had been heard to remark, "We've got a chore to do, we might as well go do it." Whereupon they rose and went to their horses. The wife of one of the men had run out into the street and had grabbed the bridle reins of her husband's horse in an effort to stop him. She said something to him, but he had tipsily spurred his horse, and the drinking partners had all ridden out of town together in the direction of the upper Largo Valley.

When word spread that Clara and Don Oliver were found dead, some of the neighbors rushed to the ranch house and cleaned up the bodies as best they could and dressed them for burial. Boards were placed on the back of Don Oliver's Model T Ford, and the bodies were placed side by side on the boards and tied down and a cover placed over them. They were then brought into town. Four inches of new snow lay on the ground, and it was so cold that decomposition of the corpses was no problem.

Henry Coleman called from Magdalena, where he was able to establish an airtight alibi, as to his whereabouts on the evening of December 11. He came to Clara's funeral in Quemado and gallantly pulled off his overshoes and loaned them to a woman so that she could walk through the mud to the small Catholic cemetery where Clara lies today in an unmarked grave.[9] Don Oliver was taken on to Magdalena and buried there.

In Socorro County Criminal Case No. 4195 is a letter from Manuel B. Otero to the Honorable Harry P. Owen, the district attorney, at Los Lunas, New Mexico. Affixed to the letter are three canceled checks written by Otero.[10] One letter reads:

> Dear Harry,
>
> I beg to acknowledge receipt of your letter of the 1st inst., asking me to send you some canceled checks when at Quemado on my return home from the ranch where Henry Coleman came in with me. I beg to comply with your request and herewith enclose the same. These two checks, one to Augustin Jaramillo for $30.00 and one to George Henderson for $1.70 were given on December 9th, as you will notice by the dates on the checks about 2 o'clock in the afternoon. We got about three miles out of Quemado and our car broke down and we had to walk back to Quemado, getting back there about 6:30 in the evening more or less. Next morning about 7:30 we left in a truck owned by Mr. John Lynch of Salt Lake.[11]

The truck was owned and operated by Joe Lynch, not John, and the story is that when Joe got ready to take off the morning of December 10 for Magdalena, Otero and his driver, Hezekiah Hall, had already made arrangements to ride with him.[12] Henry Coleman appeared from somewhere and asked for the favor of a ride, too. Joe told him that the three of them would pretty well fill up the cab of his truck, but Henry was determined to go. "I'll get me a quilt and wrap up in that and ride behind, if you'll take me," Henry pleaded. Joe let him go along. One the way in, when the truck and its passengers reached a place in the road known as Red Flats, east of Pie Town, they had the misfortune to run out of gas. Hezekiah Hall, driver of the service car that had been broken down and left at Quemado, happened to know about an old Model T Ford that had succumbed to one of the many ailments known to the Model T vintage and was sitting on a back road, about three or four miles away. He, Joe Lynch, and Henry Coleman took some wrenches and walked the distance. Lynch stayed with the truck. When they reached their goal, they unfastened the tank of the Model T that happily contained the needed gas and then walked the three or four miles back to the truck. They took turns carrying the gas tank. (Men of that time were patient and good-natured in the face of such vicissitudes, and made light of the inconveniences involved.)

The letter continues:

And [we] were all that day on the road getting into Magdalena bout 11:30 at night I should judge more or less December 10th, next morning December 11th, I gave Hez Hall the man whose car I had hired this check which I enclose for $60.00 December 11th. This is all the information I am able to give you on this subject. I have known Henry Coleman for years and he acted to me the same as he always has, he did not seem to be worried or excited in any way.

With my kind personal regards, I am,

Most respectfully,
Manuel B. Otero

With a fine abandon for banking rules, the check made out to George Henderson had been endorsed "Mrs. G. W. Henderson," and had been honored accordingly.[13]

This missive efficaciously established the whereabouts of Henry on the night of the murders, in spite of the fact that one zealous subscriber to the theory that Foster was the hired murderer told me that "he knew a man who was camped near the Rito Creek, somewhere around the night of the murders, and that he saw Foster and Coleman go back and forth within sight of his camp several times."[14] It would seem from the evidence that Henry was able to produce that it could not have been Henry that he saw that dreary and deadly evening.

There were many people, though, who thought that Henry Coleman at least hired the killer or killers. Certainly, he benefited by Clara's passing, as in due time he became executor of her estate. But when one studies the facts, it is obvious that Bourbonnaise might well have had his own motives for killing her, and it is possible that Coleman might have reaped the benefits as he saw the results rearing their heads attractively before him. So Coleman might not have had actually anything to do with the murders, as he convincingly claimed. No charges were ever brought against him or Ben Foster, the character who many swear to this day was the actual murderer. It is argued by those who adhered to the Foster theory that Ben, doubtless known before by Henry, had never been seen in the Quemado country previous to the killings, and that he suddenly appeared from nowhere.

The date of the double murder was established as the evening of December 11, and as early as December 16, a complaint made by one E. D. Oliver (a brother of the murdered Don Oliver) was sworn to and filed.[15] It read, "State of New Mexico, Plaintiff, vs. Frank Borboney, Oscar Caudill and Fred Caudill, defendants.[16] Action, murder, H. P. Owen, District Attorney, Attorney for Plaintiff. M. C. Spicer, attorney for Defendants."[17] Seldom was the name of Bourbonnaise in ensuing documents spelled correctly, or even spelled the same. The warrant was issued and delivered to Elfego Baca, the famous deputy sheriff of Socorro County.[18] Further down the page of the transcript dated January 30, 1919, 2:00 p.m., reads, "Case called, all parties present. Now comes defendants waived their preliminary hearing, through their attorney, whereupon the court fixed their bonds as follows: for defendants to await the action of the next Grand Jury: Oscar Caudill, Five Thousand Dollars, Fred Caudill, One Thousand. Bond to be approved by the sheriff." This part of the transcript was signed by a Socorro County justice of the peace, and directly beneath it was the terse notation, "January 30th, 1919, Frank Borboney was not present to this court as he was killed before trial was had."

To explain this turn of events, I will take you back to the words of the Spanish American cowboy, J., who told me that after Clara Coleman and Don Oliver were killed, he was hired to stay out at her place for a few days and look after things. Henry Coleman, who had come to Quemado for Clara's funeral, had a room permanently rented at the home of his friend Severo Lopez.[19] He did not use it too often, but he had the keys, and he liked to have it for a place to hang his hat when he was in the country. He was there the day that J. happened to go to town, riding one of the Coleman horses. J. had on Clara's chaps that day, and he left them across his saddle and put the horse into Lopez's corral. Henry happened to be in his room that day and saw the horse and noticed the chaps. He asked who was riding the horse and wearing those chaps. When he learned who it was, he called J. into his room and asked him what he knew about the killings. Both men confided in each other that they thought the murderer might have been Bourbonnaise. Henry's eyes glinted. "It's not so bad to shoot down a man," he said. "But a woman, why, it don't take any nerve to do that!" And he snorted in rage, "Why, I'll just kill the son of a bitch!"

Nearly all the accounts of how Frank Bourbonnaise met his end specify that Henry was somehow able to get a warrant for Bourbonnaise's arrest. Henry's faithful friend Felipe Padilla was the deputy appointed to issue the warrant. Together they went to present Bourbonnaise with the warrant, but Henry went over to Clara's house to wait there. It was agreed that Felipe should arrest Bourbonnaise and then take him over to the Coleman house, west of the creek.

Hardly anyone remembers the facts of what happened next. Actually, there were four men involved. The names listed on the true bill for the murder of Frank Bourbonnaise were Henry Coleman, E. D. Oliver Jr., Hugh Neighbor, and Felipe Padilla.[20] I never could find anyone who had the slightest idea of who Hugh Neighbor was, so thoroughly had the facts sunken into oblivion, but we must conclude that following his killing of Clara and Don Oliver, Henry Coleman, with characteristic persuasiveness, was able to convince the Oliver family beyond any doubt that Bourbonnaise et al. had been the killers. Once convinced, the Olivers were primed for revenge and retribution. Evidently, Hugh Neighbor was staying with the Olivers at the time of the murders and may have even been married to one of the Oliver women. I was unable to learn very many details, but I concluded that he was drawn into the affair by virtue of his proximity, and he was not connected with it through any long-standing circumstances. Evidently, he left the country soon afterward. Today, no one is certain who he was, or why he should have been named in the case. One man vaguely remembered that when Felipe Padilla went to arrest Frank Bourbonnaise, there were "some others who waited outside."

The unfortunate Bourbonnaise was in bed at his house at the time the small posse arrived. He had evidently anticipated that he might have some callers, but not with sufficient acumen to either defend himself or flee the country. His daughter answered the door and told the men that her father was sick in bed. Felipe, the deputy, went in and Bourbonnaise quickly recovered, rising from his bed at the point of a gun. He had a gun of his own above the fireplace, and he tried to grab it, but a gun was stuck unceremoniously in his ribs, and he was ushered outside. Outside, he was taken to the Coleman house across the creek, hardly a quarter mile away. He was told Henry Coleman wanted to talk to him.

It is highly doubtful if Henry, sitting in his ex-wife's kitchen, had planned on much conversation. He testified later, on trial for Bourbonnaise's murder, that there was a rifle leaning against the wall of the kitchen, and that when Bourbonnaise came in the south door, he tried to make a run for the rifle. Coming in from the bright sunshine outside, it is doubtful whether Bourbonnaise had time to see any object in the room. It is doubtful if he even had time to say a word. Henry shot him as he stepped inside.

Bourbonnaise's companions who were indicted with him for the murder of Clara Coleman and Don Oliver hastily left the country to avoid meeting the same fate. Whether Henry actually sought to avenge the death of the woman who had once been his wife or whether, as those who believe that Foster was the killer contend, he merely wanted to silence Bourbonnaise because he knew too much about the killings, no one will ever know. One fact persists: Bourbonnaise was unceremoniously gunned down. But there were four men who swore it happened just as Henry said it did (i.e., Henry shot him in self-defense).

The wording of the true bill for murder is a study in legal verbos-
ity, assaulting the eye with its jingle of words—a repetition of them—
so presented, and in such profusion, that it defies understanding
and renders the reader weary of eye and mind almost at the outset.
But I quote it, in part:

At the March term, A.D. 1919, the Grand Jurors of the State of
New Mexico, taken from the body of the good and lawful men
of the County of Socorro, in the State of New Mexico, duly
selected, tried, empaneled, sworn and charged at the March
Term A. D. 1919, of the Court aforesaid, upon their oaths do
present: That Henry Coleman, E. D. Oliver, Jr., Hugh Neighbor
and Felipe Padilla, each late of the County of Socorro, in the
State of New Mexico, on the 22nd day of December, in the year
of our Lord One Thousand Nine Hundred and Eighteen, at the
County of Socorro, in the State of New Mexico aforesaid, with
force and arms in and upon the body of Frank Bourbonnaise,
in the peace of the State then and there being unlawfully, maliciously, feloniously, willfully, deliberately and premeditat-
edly, with their malice aforethought, and from a deliberate and
premeditated design then and there unlawfully and maliciously
to effect the death of Frank Bourbonnaise, then and there did
make an assault and they, the said Henry Coleman, E. D. Oliver,
Jr., Hugh Neighbor and Felipe Padilla, in their hands then and
there had and held, then and there unlawfully, maliciously . . .

. . . and so on, and so on! But—do you get the idea?—they shot him!
That's the gist of the document, ending in a note from which all drama
has been wrested by the monotony of the jargon used to describe it:
"Frank Bourbonnaise, one mortal wound, from which mortal wound
he, the said Frank Bourbonnaise, then and there did die . . ." He did die,
then, with the meaning so pounded into the script that it had become
forever meaningless. And with the closing maxim, so overshadowing
all else that it was included in the printed form of the bill and not just
typed in—to wit, that the crime that had been committed was not so
much against the dead man and his bereaved family but "against the
peace and dignity of the State of New Mexico!"

Notes

1. Edward Clemens Wade Sr., a leading attorney in Las Cruces, was born in Barnwell, South Carolina, on January 8, 1855. Educated on the Isle of Man for six years, he became a leading attorney in Las Cruces. Wade died in Las Cruces on October 14, 1927. "Edwards Clemens Wade Jr.," *Find a Grave*, accessed July 1, 2021, www.findagrave.com/memorial/114723020/edwardclemenswade; 9th Census (1870), Brooks County, GA; 12th (1900), 13th (1910), and 14th (1920) Census, Doña Ana County, NM; *Albuquerque Journal*, October 14, 1927.

   The Missouri-born Charles Lucas Hunt Sr. was a prominent rancher at Lone, Union County, New Mexico. Hunt later moved to Missouri, where he died on March 3, 1941. *Star & Times* (St. Louis), March 4, 1941; see https://www.ancestry.com/family-tree/person/tree/112388350/person/342057373811/facts?_phsrc=tHs572&_phstart=successSource, accessed July 1, 2021. Alice Casey Hunt was born in New Mexico on May 7, 1875, and died at age 75 in Phoenix on February 6, 1953. *Arizona Republic* (Phoenix), February 11, 1953.

2. The Farr family left Scotland for Germany in the 1600s. George Farr was the first member of the family to immigrate to the United States, arriving at Cole County, Missouri, in 1818. The Farrs first arrived in New Mexico in the late 1800s and were in the mercantile business in Albuquerque for a short time. George Adam Farr homesteaded on the San Agustin Plains, east of Horse Springs. For several generations the family spoke German at home. Farr had originally managed a ranch in the Manzano Mountains and acquired property at Rosedale, southwest of Magdalena. On the San Agustin Plains, the Farrs, especially George David Farr, who was born at Carrizozo in Lincoln County in June of 1898, were able to acquire additional land from small ranchers and homesteaders. For many years the Farrs ran both sheep and cattle but eventually gave up the former for the latter. The family members were among the last cattlemen to use the Magdalena Stock Driveway to get their cattle to market, driving a large herd of cattle to Magdalena as late as 1967. Two years earlier, George Farr defied the federal government missile program by refusing to halt a cattle drive for the firing of missiles from Utah to White Sands Missile Range. The missile program had to be halted until the Farrs could get their herd to market. George and his sons, Ed and Dave, and their use of the driveway, were featured in a lengthy article in the *Albuquerque Tribune*. Dave Farr Oral History, *Catron County Historical Society Newsletter*, n.d.; 15th

Census (1920), Socorro County, NM; 16th (1930) and 17th (1940) Census, Catron County, NM; George Adam Farr, New Mexico Wills and Probate Records, April 6, 1903, Socorro County Clerk's Records, Socorro, NM; George Adam Farr World War I Draft Registration Card, Ancestry.com. *Albuquerque Tribune*, October 19, 1967, and November 18, 1974.

3. Oran Wilkes (Wilks) Sr., yet another Quemado rancher, was born at Snyder, Texas, on May 13, 1892. Wilkes was a witness for the state against Fred Caudill in the murder of Donovan Oliver and Clara Coleman. By the time the brown-eyed, brown-haired Wilkes completed his World War I draft registration card at Quemado in May 1917, he had lost his right arm. By 1920, Wilkes had moved back to Texas with his wife, Cora Elizabeth Dillingham, where he was working as a farm laborer at Post in Garza County. It was at Post that a two-month-old son died of whooping cough in September 1927. By 1930 Wilkes was at Harmony in Lea County, New Mexico, where was working on a farm with his wife and six children. By the time of World War II, Wilkes was at Bronco in Yocum County, Texas. Wilkes died on January 13, 1967, and was buried in South Park Cemetery in Roswell; 13th (1900) Census, Scurry County, TX; 14th (1910) and 15th (1920) Census, Garza County, TX; 16th (1930) Census, Lea County, NM; *Find a Grave*; World War I and World War II Draft Registration on Ancestry. com, accessed September 9, 2021. See also *State of New Mexico vs. Oscar Caudill*, April 2, 1920, Williams Papers.

4. From a Pennsylvania farming family, Edwin Edgar Engle was born in Ellston, Iowa, on October 15, 1884. According to his World War I draft card, Engle was short, stocky, and had black hair and gray eyes. In the early decades of his life, Engle lived in Union, Ringgold County, Iowa, on the Missouri border. At the age of 19 in 1904, Engle married Eugenia Mae Norman in Roger Mills County in western Oklahoma. At Sayre, Oklahoma, a son, Frederick Melvin, was born in 1905. A daughter, Edna Eugenia, followed three years later and a second daughter, Lola Mae Eugenia, followed in 1914. After working in Oklahoma as a barber, Engle moved to Quemado during World War I, and by 1920, working twelve hours a day, he was serving as the village postmaster and was operating a garage and small store. Following the death of his wife in 1918, Engle married Zora A. Blake in El Paso in November 1920. A daughter, Katherine Adela, was born in 1923. Engle died in Quemado at the age of 66 in 1950; 1910 Census, Ringgold

County, IA; 1910 Census, Beckham County, OK; 1920 Census, Socorro County, NM; 1930, 1940 Census, Catron County, NM. Edwin E. Engle family tree, Ancestry.com, accessed July 21, 2021, https://www. ancestry.com/family-tree/person/tree/75376950/person/30317473387/ facts?_phsrc=ULZ1091&_phstart=successSoure.

5. Ruins of Clara Coleman's twelve-by-eighteen-foot rock-and-adobe dugout stand today beside Largo Creek. The structure was dug into the side of a small hill on top of which once stood a small Native American ruins. A juniper hitching post remains in front of the dugout. Largo Creek, which flowed freely at the time, is dry today for most of the year, largely as a result of the construction of Quemado Lake at the head of the creek, which, along with climate change, has markedly altered the ecology along the upper creek bed.

6. Escondido Mountain, the second highest in the northern part of the county, is 9,846 feet.

7. Born on March 2, 1879, the oldest son of Pedro Baca and Selveria Piño, Epifanio Baca and his wife, Adelaida, spent their early years in Mangas. Epifanio could read and write both English and Spanish but had no formal education. Short, with blue eyes and light hair, he worked at Mangas as a sheepherder, but sometime after 1910 Baca moved to the Largo, where he was able to purchase a small 160-acre ranch. Most of the time the family lived in Quemado where Baca became the justice of the peace. 13th Census (1900), 14th Census (1910), 15th Census (1920), Socorro County, NM; 16th Census (1930) and 17th Census, (1940), Catron County, NM; World War I Draft Registration Card, Ancestry.com.

8. Born at Belton in Bell County, Texas, on October 12, 1872, James Benjamin Childers, along with his wife, Miram, and their nine children, settled on a small plot of land in Largo Canyon. Childers later moved to southern Utah and died in Las Vegas, Nevada, in August 1948; he was buried in Woodlawn Cemetery in the city. 1920 Census, Socorro County, NM.

9. Several years after Clara Coleman's death, a polished black granite marker with her name, date and place of birth, and death, was placed on her grave.

10. Manuel B. Otero, the only son of the famous Manuel Antonio Otero (1860–1881), was born on November 19, 1889, only months after his father was murdered, near Estancia. His half-sister Estella was married to Aldo Leopold and his nephew was the prominent New Mexico

Republican and sheepman Solomon Luna. Otero married Lucy Gruglia in Chicago in December 1912. His World War I draft card describes him as six-feet, one-and-one-half inches tall, stout, with brown hair and blue eyes. Otero was well known in Republican territorial politics. His uncle, Solomon Luna, had one of the largest herds of sheep in the territory and was a longtime member of the National Republican Committee. At the time more than 70 percent of the Hispanics in New Mexico identified with the Republican Party of Abraham Lincoln. Thousands had fought in either the New Mexico Volunteers or Territorial Militia during the Civil War. Otero ran a large sheep ranch west of Socorro. President William Howard Taft appointed Otero assistant postmaster of Santa Fe in 1910, and two years later Taft named him state collector of revenue. Otero married Lucy W. Gruga. Otero ran for governor of New Mexico in 1924 and newspapers throughout New Mexico proclaimed him the winner. Ten days after the election, however, the results from Quay County in Anglo- and Democrat-dominated "Little Texas" gave Otero's opponent, A. T. Hannett, 185 more votes than what was initially announced and a statewide majority of 111 votes. Otero denounced the shenanigans in counting and reporting the votes in Quay County and filed charges to overturn the results, but he eventually dropped the charges and Hannett was proclaimed governor. Otero served as collector of customs at El Paso during the administrations of Calvin Coolidge and Herbert Hoover. Active in Republican politics, Otero was a delegate to the Republican National Conventions in 1940, 1944, and 1952. A strong supporter of Dwight D. Eisenhower for president in 1952, he was predicted to be named as American ambassador to Mexico. Although a longtime resident of Albuquerque, Otero died in Santa Fe on May 1, 1963, at the age of 79, and was buried in the city's Rosario Cemetery. *Abilene* (Texas) *Reporter*, November 11, 1952; *El Paso Herald*, December 11, 1912; *Albuquerque Journal*, April 1 and August 19, 1952, and June 28, 1959; *Albuquerque Tribune*, May 2, 1963. See Ancestry.com, accessed July 22, 1921, https://search.ancestry.com/cgi-bin/sse.dll?dbid=6482&h=24078629&indiv=try&o_vc=Record:OtherRecord&rhSource=2556; Kenneth Burt, "Manuel B. Otero, Almost Governor," *Kenneth Burt's Blog*, June 23, 2015, accessed June 20, 2021.

Born in Philadelphia in 1868, Harry P. Owen obtained a law degree in night school in Chicago and came to Raton in 1889 as the agent for the Maxwell Land Grant. His World War I draft card describes him as tall with medium build, brown hair, and gray eyes. A few years later, he moved to Albuquerque and began a general practice. Active in New Mexico Republican politics, Owen was the clerk of the territorial legislature and clerk of the district court, and was appointed district judge of the Seventh Judicial District that included Socorro, Valencia, Sierra, and Catron Counties, to replace Merritt C. Mechem when Mechem was elected governor in 1920. Living in Los Lunas, Owen was elected judge in 1924 and in 1930. He married Katherine MacGillivray, who had immigrated to the United States from Canada, in Alamogordo, and the couple had two sons and two daughters. Owen retired in January 1937 after fourteen years on the bench when he was defeated by Eugene Lujan. After two years of bad health, Owen died in Albuquerque at the age of 72 on November 3, 1940, of a heart attack in his sleep. 1900, 1910 Censuses, Bernalillo County, NM; 1920, 1930 Censuses, Valencia County, NM; *Belen News* (NM), January 6, 1916, October 24, 1918, and November 14, 1918; *El Hispano-Americano* (Belen), December 30, 1916; *Estancia News Herald* (NM), November 20 and December 5, 1912, and May 15, 1919; *Sierra County Advocate* (Hillsboro, NM), August 18, 1916, October 9 and 30, 1914, and November 6, 1914; *Albuquerque Journal*, November 3, 1940; *West Schuylkill Press and Pine Grove Herald* (Tremont, PA), December 27, 1940; *Santa Fe New Mexican*, November 2, 1940.

11. In 1920 John C. Lynch was one of Henry Coleman's closest neighbors west of Salt Lake. The elderly Lynch was born near Clarksville, Texas, in 1846, the son of Thomas and Maria Lynch. Ninety-three miles to the west on November 8, 1874, at the age of 21, Lynch married Sarah Elizabeth "Lizzie" Henderson at Grayson, Texas, just south of the Red River. By age 63 John had moved with Sarah to Lovington in what was at the time Eddy County, New Mexico, where they were trying to eke out a living at farming. About the time of World War I, they headed west with their son, Roger, and homesteaded near Salt Lake, where they were able to acquire a sizeable ranch. By 1930, however, John and Sarah had moved back to Lovington, where Sarah died at the age of 77 during the Great Depression in 1930. John died five years later at the age of 89 and was buried beside his wife in the Lovington Cemetery. 9th Census (1860), Red River County, TX; 11th Census (1880), Cooke County, TX; 14th Census (1910), Eddy County (later Lea County), NM; 15th Census (1920), Socorro County, NM; 16th Census (1930), Lea

County, NM. "John C Lynch," *Find a Grave*, accessed December 24, 2021, http://www.findagrave.com/memorial/16511729/john-c-lynch.

12. Three of John and Lizzie's sons, Claude, Joseph, and Jesse, lived on a separate ranch near Salt Lake. The youngest of the three brothers, Claude, was married with two small children. At the time both Joseph and Jesse were single; 15th Census (1920), Socorro County, NM.

    Hezekiah Hall was born in Washington, D.C., on November 19, 1889, and raised in Water Canyon on the eastern slopes of the Magdalena Mountains, halfway between Socorro and Magdalena. The son of Nathan and Alice M. Hall, Hezekiah attended three years of college, probably at what was then New Mexico School of Mines, after the family moved to Socorro. His World War I draft card describes him as slender, of medium height, with black hair and brown eyes. Married to May, he was working in Magdalena as a chauffeur in 1920 and by 1930 was operating a filling station. With the election of Franklin D. Roosevelt in 1932, he was appointed postmaster in Magdalena in July 1933 and was reappointed several times. The couple had two children, Alice May, who married Jake Scott and lived in Reserve, and a son, Nathan, named after Hezekiah's father, who lived in Magdalena for several years and became a land-owner in Catron County. Hall died at the age of 76 in 1966 and was buried beside his wife in Sunset Memorial Cemetery in Albuquerque. *Albuquerque Journal*, January 15, 1952; 12th Census (1900), 13th Census (1910), 14th(1920), 15th Census (1930), 16th Census (1940), Socorro County, NM, NA. Also see Hezekiah Hall, *Find a Grave*, https://www.findagrave.com/memorial/64042613/hezekiah-hall, and https://www.ancestry.com/search/?name=hezekiah_hall&event=_socorro-new+mexico-usa_2727&birth=1889, both accessed June 9, 2021.

13. The youngest of seven children, George W. Henderson was born at Fort Union, New Mexico, on November 11, 1873, to a Welsh-born Irish mother and New York–born father who was also of Irish ancestry. Henderson was raised at Cimarron, where his father helped edit the *Cimarron News Citizen*. In Cimarron Henderson was only able to complete the fourth grade. At an early age, Henderson moved to Springerville, Arizona, where he married in 1895 and ran a small cattle ranch near Concho. By 1910 Henderson had moved to the Quemado area, where he remarried and continued in the cattle business. He is described on his World War I draft registration card as of medium

height with dark hair and blue eyes. Cruz Sanchez, fifteen years his junior, was born in the mining community of Chloride in Sierra County. Two daughters, Mary and Lucy, were born of the second marriage. By 1930 the Hendersons had moved to Long Beach, California, where George worked as a night watchman for the Richfield Oil Company. By 1940 he had moved to Flagstaff, Arizona, where he and Cruz were living with a son-in-law and their daughter, Lucy. The exact date of Henderson's death is unknown. 1880 Census, Colfax County, NM; 1900 Census, Apache County, AZ; 1910, 1920 Censuses, Socorro County, NM; 1940 Census, Coconino County, AZ; birth certificate of Lucy Henderson, Concho, Arizona, February 20, 1911, Arizona, US, Birth Certificates, 1880–1935, Ancestry.com; Marriage Certificate of George W. Henderson and May Phelps, Springerville, Arizona, November 10, 1895, Arizona, US, Marriage Collection, 1864–1982, Ancestry.com.

14. Rito Creek has its headwaters about six miles east of Quemado and runs west to join Largo Creek at Quemado.

15. Edward Dionysius Oliver Jr., who was nine years older than Donovan, was born at Weatherford, Parker County, Texas, on December 5, 1889. Short, slender, with blue eyes and light brown hair, he enlisted in the US Navy in 1908 and worked as an electrician but was discharged for unknown reasons after only four months in the service. According to his World War I draft card at Carrizozo, he was working as an automobile mechanic and claimed he had a "weak heart." In 1920 he was working in the "oil fields" northwest of Magdalena. By 1930 he was in El Paso working as a salesperson for a loan company. He completed a World War II draft card at El Paso in April 1942 at age 52; it describes him as five-foot-seven, with a ruddy complexion. He died at Brownwood, Brown County, Texas, in May of 1965 at the age of 75. 14th Census (1900), 15th Census (1910), Palo Pinto County, TX; 15th Census (1920) Census, Socorro County, NM. 16th Census (1930), 17th Census (1940), El Paso County, TX; World War I and World War II draft cards, Ancestry.com, https://www.ancestry.com/imageviewer/ collections/6482/images/005243330_01468?treeid=&person-id=&hintid=&queryId=d3e5c0df832706ec43d6c0b673041fb5&use-PUB=true&_phsrc=fsb48&_phstart and US, World War II Draft Registration Cards, 1942, Ancestry.com, both accessed July 3, 2021.

16. Oscar York Caudill said his grandfather emigrated from Spain. The original family name was said to be Caudillo, but it somehow

became anglicized to Caudill. Oscar Caudill was born to John Asbury Caudill Sr. and Catherine Frances "Kate" Brawner on April 18, 1865, in Hazard, Perry County, in southeastern Kentucky, one of the poorest areas of Appalachia, only days after the surrender of the Army of Northern Virginia at Appomattox Court House, Virginia. After the Civil War, the Caudill family moved to North Carolina and then to Palo Pinto, Palo Pinto County, Texas, west of Fort Worth. Seven children would follow. At the age of 28 in 1893, Oscar wed Caroline G. "Callie" McAdams, and three children were born of the marriage. Oscar and his first wife tried farming in Cheyenne, the county seat of Roger Mills County, Oklahoma, in the western part of the state, and then at the community of Berlin in the southeastern part of the county, and finally in Sayre in Beckham County to the south. Oscar married Hazel Clara Wilms, twenty years his junior, in Albuquerque on March 7, 1919. The couple lived at Loraine in Mitchell County, Texas, before moving to Scurry County. Eight children were born of the marriage, the youngest when Oscar was 75. In 1940 Oscar, Hazel, and their seven youngest children, ages 2 to 19, were living in a small house in Hot Springs (Truth or Consequences), rented for thirteen dollars a month. A son, Oscar Debs, was killed while serving in the 90th Infantry Division, the Tough Hombres, in the attack on German positions at St. Germain-Sur-Seves, France, on July 23, 1944, and is buried in the American Cemetery at St. Laurent. Oscar Caudill later dictated his version of the murders on the Largo to Eve Ball. Hazel died in Albuquerque on January 15, 1956. Oscar outlived his second wife by less than a year, dying in July 1957 at the age of 91. Oscar Caudill was buried beside his wife in the Quemado Community Cemetery.

In January 1972, Caudill's version of the violence along Largo Creek as he told the story to Eve Ball was published in *Frontier Times* as "Hell on the Largo." Large parts of the piece were derived almost word for word from Eleanor Williams's writings.

Oscar's brother, Frederic "Fred" Caudill, was born in North Carolina on February 12, 1868. In Oklahoma he married Rosie Caudill, and four children were born of the marriage. The youngest child, Faro Wilson Caudill, became the favorite subject for the noted Depression-era photographer Russell Lea during his extensive photography of Pie Town's homesteaders in 1940. In 1927, at the age of 59, Fred had remarried, this time to a widow, Elizabeth "Lizzie" Schalbar. While Oscar settled on the Largo, Fred and Lizzie Caudill homesteaded on the north side of Big Alegre Mountain, seven miles south of Pie Town. Fred died in Albuquerque on September 17, 1941. Lizzie would outlive her husband by more than two decades. Kathryn McKee-Roberts, *From Dust to Dust: Cemeteries in Northern Catron County* (Bosque Farms, NM: self-published, 2006), 179; *Albuquerque Tribune*, January 16, 1956; 11th Census (1880), Palo Pinto County, TX; 13th Census (1900), Roger Mills County, OK; 14th Census (1910), Beckham County, OK; 16th Census (1930), Catron County, NM; 17th Census (1940), Sierra County, NM.

17. Born in Pigeon Grove, Wisconsin, on May 9, 1972, Marion Clifford Spicer was a prominent attorney in Socorro. Married to Lydia Augusta Smith at age 22, Spicer had settled in Clovis before moving to Socorro. Spicer later remarried and moved to Los Angeles, where he died at the age of 65 on August 18, 1957. 1910 Census, Curry County, NM; 1920 Census, Socorro County, NM; *Polk's Arizona and New Mexico Pictorial State Gazetteer and Business Directory, 1912–1913* (St. Paul, MN: R. L. Polk & Co., 1912), accessible at Ancestry.com

18. The notorious Elfego Baca was born in Socorro, New Mexico, on February 10, 1865. As a child, Elfego was taken to Topeka, Kansas, but after the death of his mother in 1880, he returned with his father to Belen when his father became a marshal. Four years later, in October 1884, Baca, only 19 at the time but a deputy sheriff in Socorro County, arrested a cowboy named Charlie McCarthy in Middle Frisco (Reserve) for disorderly conduct. "I will show the Texans there is at least one Mexican in the county who is not afraid of any American cowboy," Baca allegedly said. The arrest resulted in at least thirty drunken Texas cowboys laying siege to a small jacal where Baca took refuge. Baca successfully stood off the cowboys, who riddled the small adobe picket structure with bullet holes for thirty-three hours. Baca became a US marshal in 1888, was admitted to the bar in 1894, and practiced law in Socorro and in El Paso, Texas. Through the years Baca held a succession of public offices, including county clerk, mayor, and school superintendent of Socorro County and district attorney for Socorro and Sierra Counties. Baca once bragged to an *Albuquerque Tribune* reporter that he defended thirty people for murder, only one of whom went to the penitentiary. Baca died in Albuquerque on August 27, 1945. Although Baca never tamed Henry Coleman while he was sheriff of Socorro County, he brought justice to the restless territory and state. Today, a statue on the main street in Reserve honors Baca and

his bravery. *Find a Grave,* accessed July 5, 2021, https://www.finda-grave.com/memorial7673426; Howard Bryan, *Incredible Elfego Baca: Good Man, Bad Man of the Old West* (Santa Fe: Clear Light, 1993); Alan Soellner, "Nine Lives of Elfego Baca," *Western Leather Holster,* April 15, 2019, https://www.westernleatherholster.com/6666-2/; Kyle S. Crichton, *Law and Order, Ltd.: The Rousing Life of Elfego Baca of New Mexico* (Santa Fe: Rio Grande Press, 1970); Leon Claire Metz, *The Shooters: A Gallery of Notorious Gunmen from the American West* (New York: Berkley Books, 1996); Stan Sager, *Viva Elfego! The Case for Elfego Baca, Hispanic Hero* (Santa Fe: Sunstone Press, 2009). At present the best biography remains Larry D. Ball's *Elfego Baca in Life and Legend* (El Paso: Texas Western Press, 1992).

19. Severo (Sebero) Lopez owned a small ranch a few miles north-west of Quemado. Lopez was married to Flora Baca and the couple raised eight daughters and four sons. Lopez, age 52 in 1920, came to Quemado from Los Jarales, a small settlement on the west bank of the Rio Grande, three miles downriver from Belen in Valencia County. His father, Francisco, had immigrated to the United States from Sonora, Mexico, and married Lopez's New Mexico–born mother, María Ignacia Baca. 11th Census (1880), Valencia County, NM; 15th Census (1920), Socorro County, NM.

20. Hugh Neighbor or Nabors cannot be identified with any certainty.

Eleanor Heacock Williams trick riding on her faithful horse, Sonny Boy, in the early 1930s. Eleanor Williams Papers.

Eleanor Heacock Williams posing with Sonny Boy while she was employed by Ringling Brothers and Barnum and Bailey Circus in 1935. Courtesy of Helen Cress.

Eleanor and Frank Williams in 1970. The pose was requested by a professional photographer and did not depict an actual end-of-day routine. Courtesy of Helen Cress.

The only known photograph of Henry Street Coleman was taken at the foot of a hill outside his brother's spacious El Paso home shortly before his death at the Goat Ranch in Catron County in 1921. Claude B. Hudspeth was a prominent El Paso attorney and influential Texas congressman who warned his brother not to return to Catron County. Courtesy of Barbara and Bub Adams.

Juan Cordoza poses at the grave of Clara Coleman at the small Sacred Heart Catholic Cemetery in Quemado. A longtime resident of Quemado, Cordoza worked for Henry Coleman and was one of many individuals in the small community that Eleanor Williams interviewed in her struggle to understand the life and times of Coleman. Photo by Eleanor Williams. Eleanor Williams Papers.

Only the fireplace still stands at Clara Coleman's ranch on Largo Creek south of Quemado. It was here that Clara and her hired hand, Donovan Oliver, were murdered on the frigid night of December 11, 1918. The aging cottonwood tree mentioned by Eleanor Williams still stands today just south of the ruins. Photo by Jerry Thompson.

Tombstone of Donovan Oliver at the Magdalena Cemetery. Courtesy of John Larson.

The 9,846-foot summit of Escondido Mountain, shown in the background here, overlooks Largo Canyon and the northern expanses of the Apache National Forest. Photo by Jerry Thompson.

A small community consisting of a post office and general store, as well as a few residences, was located on the east side of Zuni Salt Lake, thirty-five miles northwest of Quemado. It was here that ranchers from the area, including Henry Coleman, Salty John Cox, and Tom Curtis, often gathered. Photo by Jerry Thompson.

Part of the residence and corrals at the Goat Ranch where Henry Coleman lived with his second wife, Minnie Davis, at the time Eleanor Williams worked on her biography of Henry Coleman. Photo by Eleanor Williams. Courtesy of Helen Cress.

The juniper corral shown here at Henry Coleman's Goat Ranch was typical in the arid expanses of northwestern Catron County. Farther south, in the piñon and ponderosa pine country, pole corrals were more common. Photo by Eleanor Williams. Courtesy of Helen Cress.

Claude Hudspeth, great-nephew of Henry Coleman, poses at what is left of the corrals at the Goat Ranch in 2021. Photo by Jerry Thompson.

Texas-born, blue-eyed Thomas Merrill Curtis moved to the Quemado area during World War I. The hardworking cattleman, victimized by Coleman's rustling, headed the posse that killed Henry Coleman at the Goat Ranch on October 15, 1921. Courtesy of Barbara and Bub Adams.

Texas-born Marion Mobley "Max" Coleman was a member of the Quemado posse that killed Coleman at the Goat Ranch. A graduate of Texas A&M University, Coleman claimed that when Henry Coleman died, he was riding his stolen horse. Max Coleman was not related to Henry Coleman, although the two had once been friends. A prominent Catron County rancher who spent much of his life in Lubbock, Texas, Coleman later wrote articles and a book on his life in the Southwest. Jerry Thompson Collection.

Henry Coleman's rustling partner, Ben Foster, allegedly hid in the Goat Ranch Spring, shown here carved into the sandstone cliff at the head of a small canyon, at the time the Quemado posse killed Coleman. Photo by Jerry Thompson.

Located just northwest of the Goat Ranch, the ditch where Henry Coleman died and the hill where he rode his horse every morning is easily identifiable. Photo by Jerry Thompson.

Claude Hudspeth and his wife, Ginger, pose at the new tombstone they helped dedicate for Henry Coleman at the Magdalena Community Cemetery in 2021. Photo courtesy of John Larson.

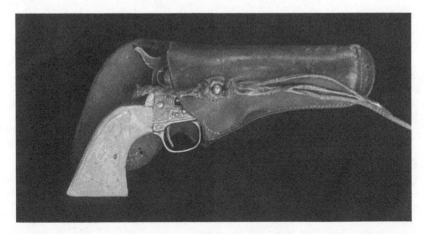

When he was found dead in the arroyo at the Goat Ranch, Henry Coleman was holding his frontier-model Colt .45 pistol that featured a steer's head carved on a mother-of-pearl handle. Rarely was Coleman seen without the pistol hanging low on his right hip. Photo by Edgar Bell, courtesy of Jerry W. Thompson Jr. Jerry Thompson Collection.

Chapter 10

Self-Defense

A ppearance bonds were filed for the four men on April 4, 1919, and each man had to post a bond of $10,000. The indictment rocked along through the spring and fall terms of court in 1919 and was finally tried and settled in January of 1920, when a written verdict of case number 4198 was penned in a large bold hand, which I believe to have been that of Judge Merritt Mechem, saying, "We the jury by direction of the Court find the defendant not guilty." This was signed by the foreman of the jury.[1]

The two murder cases were both filed on April 2, 1919, and although the Bourbonnaise murder was committed about eleven days later than the Coleman-Oliver killings, the latter dragged on a year longer than the Bourbonnaise case. It was not settled until January 4, 1921.

Much of interest is in the two old files on the Coleman-Oliver murder case, numbers 4195 and 4196, respectively. The musty old papers somehow breathed with the drama of that day, and the funny, almost childlike notations made in connection with the case contrast sharply with the everlasting monotony of the legal wordings.

The two true bills for murder abound in the same prolix style, all about how Oscar Caudill on the eleventh day of December did, with a superabundance of "saids" and "aforesaids," "unlawfully, maliciously, feloniously," and all the rest of it, do things with a "certain pistol, commonly called a revolver then and there being charged with gunpowder and diverse leaded bullets," and after an unconscionably long time, according to the descriptive talk of the legal form, "the said Clara Coleman and Donovan Oliver, then and there did die." According to the blow-by-blow account of the crime given in the true bill, it took a long time to kill those two unfortunate people!

But in these same files, sparkling against the dead wordiness of the legal descriptions, are the jotted-down words of different personages that give life and interest to the old, all-but-forgotten crime. In most cases, the ones who wrote the words remained nameless, with only their thoughts surviving the years.

A yellowing letter to Elfego Baca shines with interest and unique expression. It is dated February 22, 1919, and reads as follows:

Hon Elfego Baca
Sheriff, Socorro County
Socorro, N.M.

Dear Sir:
Referring to (our) conversation last evening, the names which have complied for which to select witnesses in the Bourbony and Coleman-Oliver cases are:
Bourbony Case
Felipe Padilla, Ed Oliver, Charles Mitchel, An old gentleman named Guyon, H. M. Neighbors, E. C. Baca, J. P., Dad Errick, Ben Foster, N. G. Baca, G. W. Henderson, Severo Lopez, O. D. Collins, J. R. Pattes, W. B. Mayfield, Mrs. George Armstrong, George Armstrong
Coleman-Oliver Case
David Simpson, Zelma Simpson, Jose Model, Doris Simpson, Orrin Wilkes, Boy named Mike at the home of Fred Caudill, Faro Model, E. C. Baca, R. E. L. Estes, S. C. Griffith, Antonio J. Baca, R. G. Foster, Mrs. Guyon and all members of the Bourbony

family, Dr. Linder, Hezekiah Hall, Niece of Fred Caudill about
11 years old, Marie Model, Steve Baca near Horse Springs, Roy
Dalton, Mrs. Oscar Caudill, Man named Barren, a freighter.
    I hope something of the truth can be learned in those matters.
                                                    Your truly yours,
                                                        (unsigned)

    If ever a person had the opportunity to read between the lines of
the written word, that opportunity—or at least the temptation—exists
in the last two names under the column of prospective witnesses for the
Bourbonnaise case. The George Armstrongs lived west of Quemado,
but the better know one of this pair was Mrs. Armstrong.[2] She was
locally famous in the role of a "wampus cat," a "wolf on wheels,"
or any other name then popular in describing a female of unbending
purpose who dearly loved a good scrap and who vied with the men of
that country in deeds both daring and shady. According to all accounts,
Mrs. Armstrong rode with a long rope handy, and she reportedly
knew how to use the rope, and often did. She was considered a rough
character. The two lists of witnesses were all typed, except for the
names of the two Armstrongs. One can clearly imagine that the person
who compiled the list was out at Quemado, doing a bit of investigating.
He had perhaps drawn up his two lists when the lady at the bottom of
list one, not wanting to be left out, arrived hurriedly, wanting to be
heard by someone of authority. She did not wish to miss out on any
chance to be in a show of any kind, and she had her husband in tow.
One can imagine that she gladly and loudly kept up her end of the
conversation, and that after she had finished, the man who was making
the lists hurriedly wrote down the name of Mrs. George Armstrong,
and was about to let it go at that when he just happened to think, "Oh,
yes. There was a Mr. Armstrong—this virago had a husband with her."
And so, he added the name, George Armstrong, as an afterthought.
    In the same file, there was a small card that looked as though
someone had scribbled on it in some haste in pencil: "Subpoena
Old Man Galwin in case of the murder of Mrs. Coleman and Oliver.
Found dead Dec. 12 1918 by Epifanio Baca—Orrin Wilkes started

with Bourbony and Oscar Caudill from Fred Caudill's to their home. Bourbony was making threats—Bourbony told Estes he was on parole from Oklahoma for murder. Roy Dalton met them—on way from Fred's to their home." There is no indication who wrote this.

Directly after the Coleman-Oliver murder, a motion was brought that appears in written form in the file in this case, dated December 17, 1918, and entitled "Application to Disinter Body." It reads as follows:

State of New Mexico
In the District Court, Socorro County

In the matter of the accusation of murder against Frank Bourbony, Oscar Caudill, and Fred Caudill."[3]

"Come now William J. Eaton, Assistant District Attorney of the 7th Judicial District composed of the Counties of Socorro, Valencia, and Sierra, and shows to the Court: that Mrs. Clara Coleman was found dead from bullet wounds, that said body was burned before a proper examination had been made to ascertain the course taken by the bullets after entering the body, that in the interest of justice, an order should be made by this Court appointing some reputable physician and directing him to disinter the body of said Clara Coleman and make such examination as may be found necessary.[4]

William J. Eaton
Assistant District Attorney

An amended document granting to the motion, repeats the facts of the case, saying:

It is now ordered by the Court that the County Physician, Dr. J. H. Linder, be and he is hereby appointed by the Court to disinter the remains of the said Clara Coleman, and make examination thereof, with all convenient speed, and to report thereon in writing to the District Attorney of the 7th Judicial District. Dated this 17th day of December, 1918

M. C. Mechem
District Judge

The Caudills left the country soon after the murders, and among the papers in this particular case is an envelope of a registered letter containing a subpoena for Fred Caudill, addressed to Belen, ordering him to appear in court in Socorro on January 14, 1920. The letter was returned unclaimed and was also marked "Unknown." Oscar Caudill did later stand trial, his codefendant, Bourbonnaise, having been removed by death from the case. But the case continued until 1921. During that year we find the last entry in case number 4196, the *State of New Mexico vs. Oscar Caudill*, dated January 4, 1921. Charges were dismissed in one brief sentence:

We the jury, by direction of the Court find the defendant Not Guilty.

Manuel A. Pino
Foreman of the Jury[5]

Notes

1. At the time Merritt Cramer Mechem was serving as a district judge for the Seventh Judicial District in Socorro. Born in Kansas, Mechem was educated at the University of Kansas and was admitted to the bar in 1893. In 1905 he became district attorney for Quay and Guadalupe Counties and in 1909 became a member of the New Mexico Territorial Council. Running as a Republican in the Harding landslide of 1920, he was easily elected governor but chose not to run for reelection. In the latter part of his life, Mechem ran a law office in Albuquerque. He died there on May 24, 1946, at the age of 75. His nephew, Edwin L. Mechem, served as the fifteenth, seventeenth, and nineteenth governor of New Mexico in the 1950s and 1960s.

2. Born in California in 1874, George Armstrong had first married when he was 30 but was divorced when he wed Nettie Shepard at Independence, Jackson County, Missouri, on March 4, 1916, shortly before the couple moved to Quemado and established a small ranch west of town. Born in Virginia in 1874, Nettie Shepard was one year younger than her husband; although she told the census enumerator in 1920 she was born in 1874, she told a census taker ten years later she was born in 1880 and was first married when she was 18. 1920 Census, Socorro County,

NM; 1930 Census, Catron County, NM; Missouri Marriage Records, 1805–2002, on Ancestry.com.

3. It should be noted that at the time the note was scribbled, Frank Bourbonnaise was still alive.

4. William J. Eaton was the son of the well-known, heavy-drinking Civil War Colonel William Ethan Eaton. The elder Eaton had come in possession or a large ranch in the Galisteo Basin thanks to his well-to-do wife, Marie Marcillene Eaton de Chavez. After the war the Eatons moved to Socorro, where he became wealthy from ranching and mining. He also headed a group of vigilantes and was active in Republican politics. The son, William J. Eaton, was born at the ranch near Galisteo on January 5, 1868. After passing the bar exam and marrying Ollie Mae Burbage in 1902, Eaton moved to Clayton in Union County. Eaton served as assistant district attorney for the Seventh Judicial District and as Socorro mayor. After working as an attorney for forty-two years, he retired in 1953 and died in Albuquerque on March 27, 1957, at age 89. 1870 Census, Santa Fe County, NM; 11th Census (1880), 13th Census (1900), 14th Census (1910), 15th Census (1920), 16th Census (1930), and 17th Census (1940), all Socorro County, NM; *Albuquerque Journal,* March 28, 1957; Thompson, *Civil War History*, 41–42.

5. Manuel Antonio Pino was born at Magdalena on October 8, 1876, and died in Magdalena on February 1, 1947. See his family tree at Ancestry com, accessed July 14, 2021, https://www.ancestry.com/family-tree/person/tree/153581242/person/222075564675/facts?_phsrc= Cmq126&_phstart=successSource. Another individual named Manuel Antonio Pino was born in San Antonio on January 31, 1886.

Chapter 11

More Shenanigans

I f it was true that Henry Coleman had nothing to do with the deaths of Clara Coleman and Don Oliver, there is no doubt that he benefited in a unique manner from Clara's passing. It certainly is a rather strange circumstance that he was able to become administrator of her estate, and that he was able to profit quite handsomely through this coup d'état. Despite the fact that Clara had relatives back in Texas, Henry Coleman wound up getting virtually all her property, both real and personal.

Henry lost no time in maneuvering to be made administrator. Consider these facts: On December 11, Clara and the luckless young man Oliver were murdered, their deaths being the very essence of the term "foul play." Eleven days later, either the killer of the pair or perhaps someone who knew too much about the murders was also killed by Henry Coleman. William Ray Morley, prominent rancher from Datil, was appointed administrator of Clara Coleman's estate.[1] But before he could ever serve in this capacity, the old files of the Probate Court of Socorro County present us with a salient bit of conniving, purporting to present everyone with lines of respectable reasonableness—a desire only to help. This strange petition reeks with what one may be sure Henry hoped would be interpreted as benign concern for his dead wife and for the fate of her estate. It reads as follows:

In the Matter of the Estate of Clara Coleman, Deceased. Comes now, Henry Coleman and respectfully represents and shows to the Court:

I: That he is a resident and citizen of the County of Socorro and State of New Mexico.

II: That on or about Dec. 11th, 1918, the above named Clara Coleman, died in said County of Socorro and State of New Mexico, that at the time of her death she was a resident of said County and State and left property to her belonging therein; that your petitioner is a creditor of the said Clara Coleman deceased and is duly qualified to act as administrator other estate, that to the best of the petitioner's knowledge and belief she left no last will and testament; that said Clara Coleman left no children surviving her and her father predeceased her, that her mother Sophia Farris was residing at Lohn, McCulloch County, Texas, and so far as petitioner is informed is still living and still resides at said place and if living is the only heir at law to said Clara Coleman, deceased; that said Clara Coleman has a sister by the name of Thirsa Bates also residing at Lohn, McCulloch County, Texas; that she also had another sister but as to whether or not she is living or as to her name or whereabouts the petitioner has no knowledge or information; that said Clara Coleman had many relatives residing in said McCulloch County, State of Texas. Your petitioner further shows the Court that an order has been made and entered in this Court appointing one William R. Morley, to act as administrator of the above entitled estate; that said William R. Morley has failed and neglected to qualify as such administrator in that he has not made oath or filed bond as required by law; that your petitioner represents to the Court that the said estate consists principally of cattle running on the range which requires immediate attention, care and control and that unless someone is appointed administrator forthwith said cattle are in danger of straying being lost or stolen. That your petitioner is informed and believes that said estate is of the value of $6,000.00; that your petitioner respectfully requests the Court to appoint G. W. Henderson as one of the appraisers of the said estate, and the Court hereby appoints A. C. Pederson as the other appraiser.

Henry Coleman, Petitioner

It might be interesting to note here that Henry had a very good idea, apparently, of where Clara's mother and sister resided. One may well wonder whether or not, since Henry felt it necessary to attend Clara's funeral, he made any effort to contact her living and closest of kin; and, if he did, one might ponder a little about why they did not come to see her laid away, or put in any claim to what little inheritance they might have had. There are many good and valid reasons why they might not have been able to come or didn't; but it is not an irrelevant thought to wonder whether or not they were even given that opportunity.

This petition was entered in the Socorro County records on January 11, 1919, one month to the day from the date on which Clara's control over her own affairs had been most effectively liquidated. On the same day, an order signed by E. B. Baca granted Henry the legal right to be Clara's administrator. It reads, "It is ordered that the said appointment of William R. Morley be and hereby is revoked and that the said Henry Coleman be and he hereby is appointed administrator of the estate of the said Clara Coleman, deceased, that before letters issue to him he take the oath required by law and file bond conditioned as required by law in the sum of $12,000."

The slick maneuvering quality of the whole deal, the power-grab strategy of it all, gives off an odor somewhat akin to the person who rubs on strong-smelling lotion over an unwashed body. In less than three weeks, the enterprising Henry had leaped all the legitimate hurdles of becoming the executor of Clara's estate, and he soon came up with an inventory that was somewhat at odds with all the verbal accounts of Clara's property. He listed her personal property as follows: "50 cows, 25 calves, 2 mules, 3 mares, 2 horses, 1 wagon, 1 set harness, 2 rooms house furniture, cash in the First Nat'l Bank of Magdalena $15.55, two notes signed by E. D. Oliver, Jr., one for $2200 and one for $800. These notes are up as security for an indebtedness of the deceased amounting to $2500 with the State Nat'l Bank of Albuquerque. This inventory completed this 30th day of January 1919."

Henry now had full authority to dispose of Clara's 440 acres, which he sold for $7,815.55, and provided receipts to the court for the sale of not only the land but also her cattle and personal effects. He even got the $15.55 that Clara had in the Magdalena bank. No mention was ever made of what he did with the two rooms of furniture.

Affixed to this final report was a list of disbursements, the expenses that Henry ran up after Clara's death. There were a great many, although several large notes signed by Clara were among them, especially one from E. D. Oliver Jr. Reading the disbursements closely, one is forced to conclude that Henry was great with details. Someone by the name of Silva worked with the cattle from time to time, and there was a marked difference between the wages paid to Silva and the wages paid to some of the other cowboys. He apparently was earning about a dollar a day. Some of Henry's old cronies, on the other hand, commanded rather imposing wages for the time in which they worked. In September of 1919, Henry's friend G. W. Henderson was paid $238 for "work with stock," and twice he was paid for appraisals. Ben Foster's wages came to $175. Henry purchased nearly $1,700 worth of cattle feed, which seems like a lot for the number of stock he listed in the inventory. When these animals were finally sold, the feed that Henry allegedly fed them came to more than half of what the animals were sold for on the market. He reported having received $3,000 for the sale of the cattle and horses. According to the market value of these cattle, no one could have stood such high running costs and remained in business for very long. There was a deficit of $3,901.75 and, in the final report, the words, "This deficit has been paid by the administrator," were entered, as the last settlement coming under what Henry described in his petition as matters needing his "immediate attention, care and control!" This closes an incredible chapter in the life of Henry Coleman. Out of its tangled and mysterious depths, public opinion has drawn a few conclusions and has presented various theories:

1. Henry hired Ben Foster to kill Clara Coleman and Don Oliver. Ben unaccountably appeared in the country at just about this time, and seemed to be so unsavory a character that the deed was readily laid at his door by a good many people. Henry then did away with Bourbonnaise because he might have known the details of the murder for hire.

2. Bourbonnaise was murdered, perhaps because he would have been able to prove his innocence and in the process throw the light back on Henry. If Bourbonnaise had established his innocence, Henry might never have been appointed administrator of Clara's estate and been able to gain control of her property. The finger of guilt would necessarily have had to point in some other direction, perhaps toward Ben Foster.

3. Bourbonnaise, either alone or aided by some of his companions who were indicated with him, killed Clara and Oliver after a bout of drinking and becoming worked up over differences between the two factions. Allegedly, he was already a paroled murderer.

4. Henry killed Bourbonnaise to avenge Clara's death and also to make the handling of her estate easier. He had convinced Don Oliver's family that Bourbonnaise was guilty and had achieved a kind of mob hysteria among friends who were with him when Bourbonnaise was gunned down.

5. Henry considered that luck had played into his hands, both in his ex-wife's death and in the fact that Bourbonnaise et al. were the suspected killers. Not averse to doing a little killing himself, he felt that everything was on his side, and that by doing a little agitating, he could easily claim that he had had to shoot Bourbonnaise in self-defense. This made it easier to gain control of Clara's estate without competition or being harassed by a close neighbor, who might have had ambitions of profiting from her demise. Just the

idea of the propinquity of the Bourbonnaise family might have
annoyed him. Henry hired Bourbonnaise to kill Clara and Oliver
and then conveniently removed him from the scene.

It is likely no one will ever know the truth. All these theories
I have listed are only conjectures, and different people have held
different opinions through the years. Actual participants in the
murders are all gone now. The due processes of law has run its course,
and the participants have been relegated to ever-dimming archival
records and newspaper articles. Many people who delve into the
history of characters like Henry have been content with speculative
innuendos and have not bothered to acquaint themselves with the
facts. Almost everything in connection with these bloody chapters
lies under the pall of the contradictory characters and their consequently paradoxical behavior. Everything simmers under sordid
possibilities and motives. One pokes tentatively at the historical
record and draws back as a faintly fetid odor starts escaping, prom-
ising a stronger stench to come!

Years give Henry his heritage of romantic color, yet it is perhaps
more fascinating over the distance of years than it actually was.

Note

1. William Raymond Morley Jr. was a legend in Catron County. He was
born at Cimarron, New Mexico, on March 17, 1876, the son of William
Raymond Morley Sr. and Ada McPherson. Morley Sr. surveyed the grade
over Raton Pass for the Santa Fe Railroad and later served as the editor
of the *Cimarron News*. Before his mysterious death in Mexico in 1883,
he invested in a large sheep and cattle ranch, the Drag-A, near Datil.
After the elder Morley's death, Ada moved her three children, Agnes,
Lorraine, and Ray, to Datil along with her new husband, who deserted
the family shortly thereafter. Morley Jr. was an all-American football
player at Columbia and the University of Michigan and coached football at Columbia. He also was one of the founders of the New Mexico
Cattle Growers Association. Morley Jr. allegedly controlled more
than two hundred sections of land, including Forest Service permits

and federal land leases. He also owned properties and businesses in Magdalena, including being a principal shareholder of the First National Bank of Magdalena. He is also remembered for building the White House in Datil Canyon. Morley's health declined for unknown reasons at the time he was appointed as the administrator of Clara Coleman's estate. He died of heart disease at Pasadena, California, in May 1932. Morley is also remembered as the father of Agnes Morley Cleveland, author of *No Life for a Lady* (1941). "William Raymond Morley Jr.," *Find a Grave*, accessed July 14, 2021, https://www.find-agrave.com/memorial/23600375/william-raymond-morley; Darlis A. Miller, *Open Range: The Life of Agnes Morley Cleveland* (Norman: University of Oklahoma Press, 2010); 15th Census (1920), Socorro County, NM; 16th Census (1930), Catron County, NM; Raymond Morley, World War I draft registration card, Cncestry.com, accessed July 10, 2021.

Chapter 12

A Trial and a Marriage

Drama follows drama in Henry's history. The trail followed by Henry, riding always on horseback and followed by his little paint pack mule, makes its hairpin turns, snakes its way through the roughs and out again into the open, leaves fresh tracks in snow and mud, and becomes impossible to follow in the rocks of mountain passes.

He was constantly on the go, and his fortunes were always in a state of flux. After selling Clara's entire holdings on the Largo for the $4,500 he listed in his final report to G. W. Blake on September 20, 1920, he received the property back from Blake within two weeks, by means of a quitclaim deed. This would make it appear that his striving to settle Clara's estate and to sell the property to settle all her debts and all the expenses incurred by him was just a little shrewd maneuvering. He must have figured on getting the land for himself the whole time. But he never lived in the house where Clara had been murdered. He had a little place north and west of Quemado, not too far from the Arizona line. This place was called Goat Springs, or just the Goat Ranch, and it was here that Henry lived after he had killed Bourbonnaise and during the time that he was being tried for murder.

I was fortunate in being able to contact an old fellow who had worked for Henry during the winter of 1919–1920. The reason why this man had been hired was because Henry had been indicted for the shooting of Bourbonnaise and was to go on trial in Socorro. Although the killing had taken place in 1918, the course of legal procedure moved slowly, and Henry went his way in freedom all this time, his bond for $10,000 having been signed for by George K. Noe, Anastacio Baca, and J. S. Baca.[1] Legend had it that his friend Severo Lopez put up his bond for the case, but the appearance bond of case number 4198 shows the owners of the above three names. Noe, Baca, and Baca were the bondsmen, and this bond was signed on April 3, 1919.

Henry, knowing that he would be gone for some time when the case was called, needed someone to look after his spread at the Goat Ranch, break the ice at the watering places for his cattle and horses, and replenish the woodpile and do other chores. Henry's hired hand, now an old man, was just a young fellow then. "I was only getting a dollar a day," he told me, "and I thought that Henry was one of the nicest fellers I ever knew. Nice to work for, never got on me if anything went wrong."

Charlie wasn't hired to ride, just to stay at the ranch and to do chores. He knew very little about Henry's cattle or how many he had. Looking back later, he said he could see that very probably Henry did not want him to know too much about it. He knew Henry's brand and saw the Flowerpot cattle as they came into the water. Henry ran the Flower Pot brand, and Clara had had the brand Diamond Ring (see fig. 12.1). Henry's lawyer brother, Claude Hudspeth, came to help in the defense at the Bourbonnaise trial.[2] When Henry returned from it, a trifle frayed, Charlie was willing to stay on. Henry did all his own riding; Charlie just did the immediate chores. When wood was needed, Charlie hitched up a couple of small horses to an old wagon and went out and gathered it. Dead wood was plentiful in the hills surrounding the Goat Ranch.

Charlie recalls that Henry had a good many horses, and that some of them were pretty badly locoed.[3] He said that when the horses

Flower Pot Brand

Diamond Ring Brand

Figure 12.1 Two brands.

came to drink, some of them were so badly locoed that they would stick their heads down outside the water trough and go through the motions of drinking but never actually get a drop. After a while they did not even come in anymore; no doubt they died. The only way that a locoed horse can be saved is to keep him in a corral and feed him; but people did not have much hay in those days, not unless they harvested the local gramma grass during a good summer, which they sometimes did.

Henry had one old blue-dappled gray saddle horse that Charlie remembers. His name was Bicycle. I have heard some men say that Henry was partial to gray horses. Bicycle was a good horse, but then it was always said of Henry, "He rode good horses."

I asked Charlie what they did for entertainment. "Well, there wasn't much to do in them days," said Charlie. Henry went to the local dances. Charlie attested to the fact that I had heard before, that Henry was quite a ladies' man. He also stated that Henry stayed dressed up, even around the ranch, neat as a pin, good boots, good Stetson hat! "Henry stood up real straight; he was a good lookin' man, a good dresser."

"What about when he had to do things like cleaning out his corrals?" I asked.

The old man chuckled. "Well, I never seen him do too much," he observed mildly. "That's what he had me for. Before me, there was another feller, an older feller. Henry was courtin' a certain lady about the time."

"Was he ever gone from the place?"

"Oh yes," said Charlie, "he'd ride off sometime an' be gone several days, maybe a week. He's never tell me where he was goin' or where he's been. But you know, I just thought he was plumb honest.

"He'd get around the house sometimes an' sing, sing by the hour. I liked to hear him. He had a right good singin' voice, an' he'd sing mostly cowboy songs. He knowed a helpin' of songs, Henry did. No, he didn't have no gee-tar; no musical instrument of any kind. Sometimes Tom Summers, a neighbor, he's come by; an' he was quite a singer too.[4] People entertained themselves that way in them days."

That was quite a different picture of Henry. And I could not help thinking: if Henry had been born twenty or twenty-five years later, with his good looks and his good singing voice, and the country shrunken so much by roads and the ubiquitous automobile, he might have become a Western star—another Gene Autry, singing his way to fame, and wearing his clothes so gracefully, and making love to the stars and starlets! Maybe, then, Henry would not have had to make his way as a lone wolf. He was smart enough; he could have capitalized on his looks, his natural sense of elan, his musical ability. Hollywood might have paid homage to him, and he would not have had to ride down into Old Mexico to dodge the harvest of his daring deeds. Poor Henry Coleman, born just a little too early for one career, and too late, really, for the kind of man he truly was! But then I thought, too, that if he had been born a little later and had not been able to escape a whole host of conventions that would have shaped him so differently, he would have been no match for the man that he actually was, could never have hoped to compare with the wealth of resourcefulness and cunning that was his in such rich measure—the eye that never missed a sign, the hand that could pull a gun like greased lightning, the tough enduring that could stay in the saddle for days on end without tiring, the mind that could outwit almost anyone, even though it was hardly even in a good cause!

But to get back to Charlie; once Henry sent Charlie and Ben Foster in to Wolf Wells, just west of Magdalena, with a little herd of goats. The goats were sold to Shorty Landavaso, and Charlie and Ben drove them all the way.[5] "Don't know whose goats they really was," said Charlie. "Ben—I didn't like him too well. He was really a meaner man than Henry." The stories all tally out pretty well; Ben never had the name of being coolly brave like Henry. Ben was a killer all right, so they all said, but he'd be more apt to shoot a man in the back. He wasn't the skilled gunman that Henry was. That Henry—he could beat most men to the draw, and they knew it and didn't fool with him. Henry didn't have to shoot from ambush; he could stand right up in front of a man and give him the start, and then beat him pulling his gun.

Charlie described him as an amiable, congenial companion. He had many friends. One close neighbor was Hamp Eaves.[6] "Hamp always said that Henry was one of the best neighbors he ever had, and one of the biggest outlaws. He knew a heap more about Henry that I did."

"Henry remarried during the spring of 1920."[7] Said Charlie, "When he married Minnie, then he didn't need me no more. That's when I left and went into Arizona and got me a job. Then's when I started hearing things about Henry. I just couldn't hardly believe it, but I heared so much from so many that I figgered some of it had to be true."

Henry chose to marry Minnie Davis under his right name. The application for their marriage license, the license itself, and the marriage certificate all show that he gave his name as Henry Coleman Hudspeth of Quemado, New Mexico, and his age as 49. His bride was Minnie C. Davis, age 31.[8] The name of Hudspeth stans out a bit ludicrously among all his repeated signatures in court under the other name, and the name of Coleman used over and over again, in business transactions of different kinds, both before and after the marriage. He must have been giving in to a bit of sentiment when he used his right name at the time of his marriage. Another thing: his trial for Bourbonnaise's murder had taken place about two months before, and it was probably known that the lawyer who helped to defend him, Claude Hudspeth, was his brother. Perhaps Henry took a good deal of pride in the cleverness and gentlemanly bearing of his brother, and his feelings about it incited him to use the family name in such a matter as marriage, rather than a name that he had hidden behind for years. It is lots more fun to attribute his motive to something highly romantic, and it might just be true!

The house where Henry and his wife lived at the Goat Ranch was built of rocks. It sat up against rock bluffs and in a small open canyon that ran upward into the bluffs and was ringed around by them. The place had a wonderful spring of water that ran directly out of the base of the rock bluff above the house. Someone, perhaps Henry, had hacked out quite a tunnel in that sandstone and had boarded up the entrance so that inside there stood three or four feet of spring water for a distance horizontally of fifteen or twenty feet inward. The rock ceiling sounded a continuous tune of drip-dripping water, and that water was piped down to the corral, into a tank or trough. The corral was a big one built of cedar posts wired close together—the old-time "picket" corral—a painstaking example of the handwork of man.[9] There was very little expense involved in picket fences, other than the work of cutting the posts and wiring them together. A man who was good with an ax could chop forty or fifty posts in a day; an exceptionally good worker may have been able to cut more than that. Only a very few years ago it was still possible to see the old pieces of rawhide that Henry used when he made the corrals at the old Record place—his first home in the Quemado country. The story I heard was that Henry moved the poles from the old Slaughter headquarters and made them into a picket corral, tying the poles together with rawhide instead of wire. The corral at the Goat Ranch may have been made in the same way, but by now most of the rawhide would have been replaced by wire. But it is interesting to know how the early settlers made so many things out of articles that they fashioned themselves, and that were not factory made. For instance, I know of one old homestead where the builder carved a doorknob and latch out of wood. So many of them were extremely ingenious in makeshift devices and clever little inventions. They had to use just what they had, and often they did not have much. The wonderful part about them was that not having something never seemed to dismay them. They always found ways of getting around a lack of anything and of making something else do!

Of course, Henry had lived at the Goat Ranch before he brought his bride there; it had been his headquarters for several years. Legend has it that the marriage itself was consummated in Quemado on March 26, 1920, and that the little town thrilled to the excitement of such a romantic episode. Mr. E. E. Engle, who had built the home on the Largo for Clara Coleman, "stood up" for the couple, as did O. D. Collins, the man who ran Quemado's little hotel and who was also in the sheep business. In fact, the marriage ceremony was held in Mr. Collins's hotel, and quite a few of Henry's friends attended. The Goat Ranch must have been an ideal honeymoon spot; it would be hard to find a more isolated place, or one farther off the beaten trail.

North of the corral was a small bare hill, a kind of a point, and it was Henry's habit to ride up on this little hill the first thing in the morning and take a look around. An old trail still shows the way he usually went; it leads from the old corral upward across an open slope to the steeper lookout above it. One of the old-timers who knew Henry said that before he got on his horse, he would always stop a moment and roll a cigarette, scanning the immediate landscape as he did so. Henry was a very careful man.

I want to quote what a very reliable old-time resident had to say about the ownership of the Goat Ranch where Henry and Minnie lived. He said,

> The Goat Ranch spring belonged to Harris Miller when we came to the country. Harris was living there at the time. It has always been my opinion that Harris had acquired the forty acres of 'script' land from Santa Fe to cover this spring. But, due probably to an error in the surveying, they missed the spring with these forty acres. A Mexican filed on one hundred and sixty acres that did cover the spring. Henry moved some cattle down there and, since no one was living there, he moved into the house.
>
> About this time, Harris had to take all of this property back, along with the cattle he had sold. Harris had a couple of lawyers take this into court. The court ruled that Harris had bought and paid for something in good money and good faith and did not get what he thought he was getting. So the government canceled the forty acres (out of the one hundred and sixty that the Mexican had filed on) and gave Harris a title to the forty that covered the spring. It seemed to be everyone's opinion that Henry had the Mexican file on these one hundred and sixty acres; don't remember the Mexican's name.

Notes

1. The Omaha, Nebraska–born George Kristead Noe was a prominent Socorro County cattle raiser. Of medium build and height with black hair and blue eyes, according to his World War I draft registration card, Noe was born on September 9, 1887, and was married with two children. He appears to have also established a brokerage business in Mexico. World War I Draft Registration Card and Passport Application, Ancestry.com., accessed December 23, 2021.

    Anastacio Baca, who was born in 1860 and raised at Jacales, just south of Belen in Valencia County, was a prominent Quemado cattleman with land east and west of Quemado. With his wife, Porfiria, whom he married in 1886, Baca also operated a sheep ranch near Mangas.

10th Census (1870), Valencia County, NM; 11th Census (1880), 13th Census (1900), 14th Census (1910), and 15th Census (1920), Socorro County, NM; 16th Census (1930) and 17th Census (1940), Catron County, NM.

Joseph Simon Baca was the sheriff of Socorro County from 1917 to 1918 and 1923 to 1924. Baca was born in Socorro on January 17, 1884, and married Enriqueta Baca in 1901. Five daughters and a son were born to the marriage. Of medium height and build with gray eyes and dark hair, Baca sold insurance at an early age before becoming one of Socorro's leading "grocerymen." After two terms as sheriff, he served on the Socorro city commission, and in 1930 he was in Albuquerque working for the State Corporation Commission. An assistant pastor of the Methodist Church of Socorro, Baca died in Socorro at the age of 68 on May 19, 1952. 14th Census (1910), 15th Census (1920), 17th Census (1940), Socorro County, NM; 16th Census (1930), Bernalillo County, NM; World War I draft registration card, Ancestry.com, accessed July 11, 2021; *Albuquerque Journal*, May 23, 1952; "A Listing of Sheriffs in Socorro County, NM," USGWArchives.net, accessed July 12, 2021, http://files.usgwarchives.net/nm/socorro/history/sheriffs.txt.

2. Claude Benton Hudspeth was the youngest brother of Henry Coleman. He was born in Medina County, Texas, the fourth son of Henry Street Hudspeth and Elizabeth Ann Hudspeth on May 12, 1877. He would say that his entire education consisted of three months in the family's log cabin on the Medina River. He worked as a cowboy, rancher, and newspaper publisher. In 1926 Hudspeth drove 1,400 head of cattle from Crockett County to a ranch in Brewster County. Hudspeth was elected to the Texas House of Representatives in 1902 and the Texas Senate in 1906. He also represented Texas in the US House of Representatives from 1919 to 1931. In Washington Hudspeth was a vocal supporter of American intervention in Mexico and once referred to Venustiano Carranza as "that spineless cactus of Mexico." He died in San Antonio on March 19, 1941, and was buried at Ozona. Kohout, "Claude Benton Hudspeth"; Claude Benton Hudspeth Papers, Special Collections, University of Texas at El Paso Library (hereafter cited as Hudspeth Papers).

3. Locoweed is a widespread poisonous plant problem in the western United States. A flowering plant called Astragalus produces swainsonine, a phytotoxin harmful to livestock. Cows and horses will sometimes seek out the plant and, as a result, develop a medical

condition known as locoism. Neurological damage can be irreversible. Cattle consuming locoweed at a high altitude, such as in western New Mexico, can die from congestive heart failure. Elk and mule deer also consume locoweed.

4. Tom A. Summers came to the Quemado area from Texas in 1912 and settled on a cattle ranch near Red Hill. Influential in the state Democratic Party, he served as deputy warden at the state penitentiary in Santa Fe from 1914 to 1933. Returning to Catron County, he was elected sheriff and served until Governor John Miles appointed him chief of the New Mexico State Police in February 1939. Summers served in that capacity until he was replaced in 1943. He died on June 12, 1944, at age 62 while visiting his son in Farmington. His wife, Minnie Lee Summers, died in Albuquerque on June 30, 1954, as the result of an automobile accident eighteen miles south of Belen eleven days earlier. After services in the Church of Jesus Christ of Latter-day Saints, she was buried in Springerville, Arizona, beside her husband. *Albuquerque Journal*, June 13, 1944, June 21, 1954; *Albuquerque Tribune*, July 1, 1954; *Catron County News*, June 24, 1938, March 9, 1939; *Farmington Times Hustler* (NM), July 7, 1944; *Gallup Independent*, June 13, 1944; 15th Census (1930), Catron County, NM.

5. Wolf Wells is in west-central Socorro County on Bureau of Land Management land about fifteen miles west of Magdalena near the Montosa Ranch.

6. Coke Hamilton "Hamp" Eaves was born at Woodbury, Texas, on August 9, 1882, died in Grants, New Mexico, at the age of 83 on December 20, 1965, and was buried in Grants Memorial Park. At 14 Eaves came to New Mexico and settled near Lovington before moving on to the Quemado area in 1907. In 1920 he was foreman of the large Fernandez Company sheep and cattle ranch near Salt Lake, where he came to know Henry Coleman. He is enumerated on the census at the time as married to Rebecca Eliza "Obie" Klepper, eight years his junior, and with two children, Johnie May and Lorenzo M. His World War I draft registration card describes him with blue eyes, light colored hair, and of medium height. Eaves later married Marie Kaiser Eaves in 1947 and purchased a cattle ranch near Ambrosio Lake. A "cow puncher by trade," Eaves took pride in being one of the founders of the Grants Rodeo in 1928. 14th Census (1920), Socorro County, NM. See obituary, photo, and miscellaneous newspaper clippings on *Find a Grave*, https://www.findagrave.com/memorial/130252026/coke-hamilton-eaves;

see World War I draft registration card and other biographical information at https://www.ancestry.com/search/?name=coke+hamilton_eaves
(both accessed February 4, 2021).

7. Marriage Certificate, Henry Colman [*sic*] Hudspeth and Minnie C.
   Davis, March 22, 1920, Socorro County Clerk's Office, Socorro, NM.
   The ceremony was performed before Justice of the Peace E. C. Baca in
   Quemado. Baca accidently reversed the birth dates of Coleman, age 49
   (February 20, 1871), and Davis, age 31 (May 10, 1888).

8. Thirty-year-old, Texas-born Minnie C. Davis is enumerated on the
   1920 census at Quemado as divorced and renting a house. She may
   be the 8-year-old orphan living with her grandparents in Robertson
   County, Texas, in 1910. A Minnie Davis or Minnie Coleman cannot be
   located in the census after her marriage, either in 1930 or 1940. 15th
   Census (1920), Socorro County, NM.

9. Although the ranch house has long since disappeared and the spring has
   little water, the picket fence constructed of juniper trees still stands at
   the Goat Ranch in the sandrock hills west of Salt Lake.

Chapter 13

Indictments without End

In all the different stories that I have gotten about Henry Coleman, I am quite aware of one thing—namely, that people who had no cattle themselves enjoyed the contacts with his undoubtedly nice personality, without having to taste the bitter fruits of property lost, strayed, or stolen.

The stealing went on, and on, and on! One person said of Henry, "He stole cattle on such a large scale that finally it wasn't safe for him to stay in the country." The gentle people around Quemado preferred to be friendly with Henry; they didn't want him for an enemy. But Henry's depredations were getting too costly to Quemado residents; and, as I have stated before, he may have grown careless. Instead of taking stolen cattle to Zuni and having them butchered and the hides and brands disposed of, so that no evidence would exist, he started branding cattle out and letting them run near Zuni under the surveillance of some of his friends. That opened the way toward "getting the goods on him." I have said that some of these later cattle were found, and therein lies a tale.

A rancher and his father who lived near the Arizona line were out doing their chores one morning when they saw two heads pop up on the skyline. The heads belonged to two riders, and soon they recognized the pair as two men whom they knew, and the men in the corral yelled out in fun, "Come on, we'll give up!" These two men were hunting cattle that Henry Coleman was supposed to have stolen, and rumor had it that these cattle were being run in the Zuni country. They rode on, and they found some of the cattle. With this feat accomplished, and cattle that Henry had actually taken rebranded, warrants were eventually issued for the stolen cattle. But first the scouts reported their finds to some of the men who had lost cattle.

Two brand new Model T Fords were commandeered to bring interested people out to check on the findings. Milt Craig ran a kind of a long-distance taxi service in Magdalena, and it was in his taxis that the men came.[1] Some of them were men who had been losing cattle and wanted to see if they could find them, and one of the drivers was Dwight Craig, brother to Milt.[2] In order to get into the country where the cattle had been seen, the Fords had to climb up some pretty formidable-looking bluffs. The same ranchers who had witnessed the vanguard on horseback saw the Fords when they came and told them cheerfully, "Hell, you can get up there, we made it a few days ago!" When the cars came back, they admitted to having had a very hard time conquering those bluffs; but, they said, they did see a few of the cattle they had been looking for.

As a result of this foray, Henry was served with a warrant on February 24, 1921. The true bill was made out against Henry Coleman by George (G. W.) Henderson, accusing the pair of "larceny of neat cattle," twelve head altogether. Four head supposedly had belonged to Nazario G. Baca and were reported stolen on October 24, 1919. Another four head, supposedly taken the same day, had belonged to Nazario Baca and Francisco Zamora, and another four were the "goods, chattels and property of some person and person to the Grand Jurors aforesaid unknown."[3] Anyway, Henry was supposed to stand trial for this affair on March 21, 1921. To cinch his appearance, two of his good Spanish American friends stood his bond in the amount of $2,500 apiece. One bondsman was Damian Padilla and the other was G. E. Sanchez, both of Socorro.[4]

The indictment, case number 4320, was the first one of what turned out to be a whole epidemic of indictments. Nine indictments followed, numbered from 4313 to 4322. Evidence had been collected systematically and patiently, and the indictments were made out at about the same time, since all of them had the date returned listed as March 26, 1921. But the thefts covered a period of two years or more, some of them going back to 1919. All but bills number 4319, 4320, and 4321 were listed as the *State of New Mexico vs. Henry Coleman and Ben Foster*, and such true bills goes into a little more detail by describing Henry as "Street Hudspeth, alias Henry Coleman." The three bills, numbers 4319, 4320 and 4321, were against Henry and George W. Henderson jointly.

Indictment Number	Taken on	No. of Cattle	Owner of Cattle
4313	May 15, 1920	1 head	E. J. Winsor
4314	Nov. 14, 1919	2 head	Oscar Caudill
4315	May 20, 1920	8 head	Suzana Armijo de Sanchez, executor of the estate of Juan Sanchez y Vigil
4316	Nov. 10, 1919	1 head	Tom Curtis
4317	May 20, 1919	16 head	M. M. Coleman
4318	Nov. 6, 1919	2 head	E. W. Myers
4319	Nov. 8, 1919	12 head	H. H. Lisle
4320	Oct. 24, 1919	4 head	Nazario G. Baca
	Oct. 24, 1919	4 head	Nazario G. Baca and Francisco Zamora
	Oct. 24, 1919	4 head	Unknown person or persons
4321	Nov. 5, 1919	1 head	J. S. Putman
4322	May 8, 1919	2 head	Isabelle Guyon; Amelia, Lola, and A. T. Bourbonnaise

I wondered why every indictment listed the charge of "Larceny of Neat Cattle." My imagination was intrigued by a rather confused image of tidy little animals being driven off, but when I looked up the meaning, my dictionary had one definition of "neat" as meaning "cattle of the ox kind, as distinguished from horses, sheep, and goats." So apparently this term comes to us from early America or even from the courts of England, perhaps, and just means "cattle and nothing else."

The case number 4320 stands alone; it was the only one in which a warrant was served on the person of Henry Coleman. In the case files of number 4317, *State of New Mexico vs. Henry Coleman and Ben Foster*, there appears a warrant for the arrest of Street Hudspeth, alias Henry Coleman, but the back of the warrant, which is always filled out upon the arrest of the person named, had never been completed. Affixed to the warrant was a typed reason for this, which reads:

This write came to hand on March 29th, 1921, and was executed by me, by making a complete and diligent search for the within named defendant, Street Hudspeth alias Henry Coleman in my County and also throughout the State of New Mexico, and I do here by certify that I have been unable to find him.
Witness my hand this 4th day of April, A. D. 1921
V. V. Tafoya, Sheriff[5]
by Nep Torres, Deputy

In the files of case number 4319, *State of New Mexico vs. Henry Coleman and George W. Henderson*, a similar notation is affixed to the warrant for Henry. It says:

This is to tertiary that within warrant was placed in my hands the 29th day of March, A. D. 1921. That within named defendants was unable to be found in this state and therefore could not be taken into custody. Witness my hand this 18th day of April, A. D. 1921.
V. V. Tafoya, Sheriff
by Nep Torres, Deputy

Henry had made the highly dishonorable act. He had vamoosed into Mexico, leaving his bondsmen, Damian Padilla and G. E. Sanchez, holding the sack. His codefendant, George W. Henderson, was served with three different warrants on March 19, 1921, and stood trial in April of the same year. His attorney, A. A. Sedillo, presented Judge Harry Owen with ten requested instructions to the jury, most of which said that viewing different pieces of evidence brought out the fact that Henry and Henderson had driven some cattle up toward Zuni and had left them in the pasture of one William H. Bossom, and that Henry had been paid by check for the cattle and had afterward endorsed some checks over to Henderson, so the jury must be sure that there was actually a conspiracy between Coleman and Henderson.[6] It was admitted, apparently, that Henry was guilty of larceny, but the lawyer was able to convince the jury that his client, Henderson, was not necessarily involved in the theft and that he had not done anything actually unlawful himself. Henderson was found not guilty on April 19, 1921.

Apparently Ben Foster was able to make himself as scarce as Henry, because there is no record of his ever having been served with a warrant, and he never stood trial. So those eleven indictments for cattle stealing have languished in the old Socorro County files for all these years, and nothing came of them.

Notes

1. Samuel Milton Craig was born in Louisiana on December 13, 1876, and died at Albuquerque on June 13, 1946. He is buried in the Magdalena Community Cemetery. Craig is listed on the 1885 New Mexico census as age 8, son of Sam M. Craig and Sally Craig, and with an older sister and four younger siblings. His World War I draft registration card indicates he was of medium build, with medium height, light hair, and gray eyes. With only a third-grade education, Craig was well respected in Magdalena and Catron County for his mechanical abilities and his car rental service. Late in life Craig moved to Gallup, where he gave his occupation as a "manager" and told the census enumerator he was making $1,000 a year, owned his own house, and was working

ninety-one hours a week. 14th Census (1910), 15th Census (1920),
16th Census (1930), Socorro County, NM; and 17th Census (1940),
McKinley County, NM; World War I draft registration card, Ancestry.
com, accessed July 16, 2021; 1885 New Mexico Territorial Census,
Ancestry.com, accessed July 16, 2021.

2. In 1900 Texas-born 21-year-old Dwight Andrew Craig was living in
Gallup with his mother and his 20-year-old wife, Maud Chrisolm, and
working as a miner. He was born on January 25, 1879, in Texas. By 1920
he had moved to Magdalena, where he was working as a butcher and
living with his wife and three daughters, Georgia, Elizabeth, and Agnes
Helen. A son, Dwight Jr., was born in 1912. By 1930 Dwight and Maud
had moved to Oilfield, Eddy County, New Mexico, where Dwight
worked as a foreman on a large ranch, supervising seven cowboys.
By 1940 Craig had moved to Gallup, where he was the undersheriff for
McKinley County. He died in 1956 and was buried in the Fort Sumner
Cemetery in De Baca County. 14th Census (1910), 15th Census
(1920), Socorro County, NM; 16th Census (1930), Eddy County, NM;
17th Census (1940), McKinley County, NM.

3. Nazario Garcia Baca was appointed Quemado postmaster in 1908 and
served in that capacity for many years. Baca was born at Belen on
March 23, 1883, and married Clara Bustamante at Riley in Socorro
County in January 1885. His wife died of the Spanish flu in 1918,
one of many Quemado-area victims. Baca died on December 6, 1922,
not long after posting Coleman's bond. The Bacas' son, Eliseo, who
lived and ranched at Mangas for many years, served as the unofficial
Quemado town historian for several years. 13th Census (1900), 14th
Census (1910), and 15th Census (1920), Socorro County, NM; Post
Office appointments and Nazario Garcia Baca family tree, Ancestry.
com, accessed July 28, 2021.

Like several Quemado Hispanic cattle and sheepmen, Francisco
Zamora, who was 57 when he signed Coleman's bond, got his start at
Mangas, the center of the sheep industry in the western part of the state,
where he married Francisca Alderete in 1880. 14th Census (1910), and
15th Census (1920), Socorro County, NM.

4. For several decades, Damian Padilla Sr. was a central figure in Socorro
County political circles. Born at Lemitar on January 18, 1889, he married
Nellie Bourguet, daughter of a Civil War veteran who had settled in the
village. The couple raised three sons and one daughter. His World War
I draft registration card describes Padilla as tall, of medium build, with

black hair. At the time he was working for the sheriff, J. S. Baca, as a county jailer. By 1920 he was with the mounted police. Padilla later moved his family to Socorro, where he worked for the city water superintendent for more than a decade reading water meters. Padilla served as a Democrat precinct chair in Socorro for sixteen years, and he spent a decade on the State Penitentiary Board and six years with the State Land Office. He died in Socorro at age 63 from heart failure and was buried in San Miguel Cemetery. 15th Census (1920), 16th Census (1930), and 17th Census (1940), Socorro County, NM; World War I draft registration card, Ancestry.com, accessed September 22, 2021; *Albuquerque Journal*, February 19, 1952.

Geronimo Eduardo Sanchez was born at Cañada Alamosa, on the west bank of the Rio Grande, thirty-two miles south of Socorro, on August 26, 1875. In 1897 Sanchez married Maria Ursula Chavez, and eleven children were born of the marriage. By 1900 Sanchez had moved to Hillsboro, the county seat of Sierra County. By 1917 he was in Socorro listing his occupation as that of a stock raiser. His World War I draft registration card describes him as of medium height, of stout build, with brown eyes and black hair. In 1930 Sanchez was in Los Angles, California. He died in Colorado on December 5, 1930. World War I draft registration card, Ancestry.com, accessed June 26, 2021; 13th Census (1900), Sierra County, NM; 1885 Territorial Census, Sierra County, NM; 11th Census (1880), 15th Census (1920), Socorro County, NM; 16th Census (1930), Los Angeles, CA; Geronimo Eduardo Sanchez family tree, Ancestry.com, accessed July 11, 2021, https://www. ancestry.com/search/?name=geronimo+eduardo_sanchez&event=_ socorro-new+mexico-usa_2727&event_x=_1-0&location=2&name_ x=1_1&priority=usa.

5. V. V. Tafoya defeated the controversial Elfego Baca for sheriff of Socorro County in a hotly contested election in 1920. Tafoya operated a pool hall at San Antonio and then Socorro. He remained active in Socorro county politics and was elected as a Democratic presidential elector in 1936 but died a few days before Franklin D. Roosevelt defeated Alfred E. Landon. 15th Census (1920), and 16th Census (1930), Socorro County, NM; *Albuquerque Morning Journal*, December 21, 1919; *Deming Headlight*, September 4, 1936; *Albuquerque Journal*, December 15, 1936.

6. Antonio Abad Sedillo was born in Socorro on April 15, 1876. Sedillo married Gertrude Vigil, who died in 1927. He was a public

school teacher, principal, and Socorro City Clerk before becoming
district attorney for Socorro, Sierra, and Valencia Counties in 1903.
Sedillo later moved to Albuquerque, where he continued to practice
law and at one time became speaker of the New Mexico House of
Representatives. He died of a heart attack at age 57 in Albuquerque
on October 24, 1933. 13th Census (1900), Socorro County, NM;
14th Census (1910), 15th Census (1920), and 16th Census (1930),
Bernalillo County, NM; World War I draft registration card on Ancestry.
com, accessed August 4, 2021; A. A. Sedillo family tree at https://
www.ancestry.com/search/?name=antonio+a._sedillo&event=_
new+mexico-usa_34&event_x=_1-0&name_x=_1; *Albuquerque Journal*,
October 25, 1933.

Chapter 14

Death at the Goat Ranch

I n writing the last chapter in the career of Henry, I am going to risk repetition by giving the accounts, verbatim, of the different narrators who told the same stories just a little bit different. By doing this we can perhaps come by a clearer conglomerate picture of Henry, of what people thought of him, and of what really happened. I will name these different accounts by number, and they are all quotations in the words of the different narrators.

> Another time, Henry was scheduled to be tried in Socorro for stealing cattle and another Mexican friend down there put up his bond. This time it really looked as though they had the goods on him. But Henry slipped off to Mexico and jumped his bond. His friend, the bondsman, knew about where he was, so he went down after him and tried to talk him into coming back. Henry threatened him and ran him out of there, and the bondsman had to pay off. His brother, a Texas lawyer, came to help in his defense the first time, but he never showed up again.

I was rather confused about why the Texas Panhandle Cattle Sanitary Board was reportedly called on in order to legally get action against Henry on one cattle stealing charge. I was set right on this by the following account:

There used to be a fellow named Bob Hilton in the country. He had stolen some cattle from Texas and had driven them into New Mexico. He took them over into the Mimbres country and held them there.

But before he could dispose of them, Henry stole them from him, and took them up around Zuni, where he had been holding quite a few of the cattle that he stole. This was lucky for Hilton, because he probably would have had charges brought against him, but when it was found where the cattle were and who had them, a warrant was issued for Henry and brought in my two Texas officers, a fellow by the name of Tipton, who was a tall slender fellow, and a shorter, heavyset man by the name of Roberts.

They came to Magdalena and looked up Dwight Craig, who was a deputy there. They wanted him to go with them out to the Goat Ranch where Henry was living then. Henry didn't own the ranch; it belonged to Harris Miller and Henry was allowed to stay there.

Well, as I said, Dwight went along to help serve the warrant. This was not one of the Socorro County warrants that were listed in the last chapter. He didn't want to go because he was a friend of Henry's, but for that very reason he finally agreed to go along. "I might be able to help Henry," he told someone. "I might be able to see to it that no dirty work is done."

The two Texas law officers were in one Model T Ford and Dwight was in another one. Both cars belonged to Milt Craig, who rented out cars. The three set out, and it was a long trip, probably close to 150 miles, over roads that were all unpaved in that day, and very rough. In due time the cars chugged up into the small canyon and pulled up in front of the house where Henry and his wife lived.

The Texas men called out for Henry Coleman. He stepped outside, and Dwight told him what it was they wanted. Tipton and Roberts climbed out. Roberts, a heavyset man and kind of a slow-moving fellow, was in front, and the taller man, Tipton, was behind. Tipton was a little more of the active type. Dwight figured that Tipton might have it in his mind to shoot Henry down from behind, so Dwight got out in front of them both and got up close to Henry so that he would be between them. He did not think that any shot would be fired under the circumstances, and none was.

The two officers demanded that Henry hand over his gun. Henry looked at them for a minute without saying anything, and then said, "If you want me in town, I'll be in as soon as I can go get a neighbor woman to come and stay with my wife. In the meantime, if you want my gun, I'll give it to you. But boys, I'm telling you now, it'll be smoking!"

The Texas men thought this over. Dwight offered them a little advice about then. He would stay and come in with Henry, he told them. And they'd better listed to him about the gun, because he could kill them both if he wanted to, before either one of them could fire a shot."

If this account is more accurate to the letter than the subsequent one, then it is a good example of the code of honor peculiar to outlaws of that day, and earlier. Then, a man's word was his bond, and it wasn't the first time that a man under arrest, and maybe charged with quite a serious crime, had said that he would show up at the required time and would keep his appointment.

But I have another account to offer, slightly different, about the same incident.

The time Dwight came out to help Roberts arrest Henry, his brother Milt had several "service" cars which he hired out; kind of long-distance taxis they were. Roberts and his deputy hired Dwight to drive them out there in one of these. Dwight didn't much want to go, but he told someone he was a good friend of Henry's, and he figured that if he went along he could see to it that Henry would not meet up with any foul play, such as getting shot down on sight.

When they reached their destination, Henry was home, but when they called to him to come out, he wouldn't go. So Dwight went in and told him that he might as well come on out, that he'd have to come and be tried sooner or later. After a short conversation, Henry agreed to go. The Texas deputies demanded, then, that he get in and go with them immediately, and that he hand over his gun. Henry assured them that he would do neither. First, he said, he and Dwight would drive down to a neighboring ranch, a few miles away, to get a woman he knew to come and stay with his wife during his absence. As for his gun, he would just keep it right where it was, on his own person. The deputies finally agreed to this and Henry went after the neighbor woman, unaccompanied by the two members of the Texas Sanitary Board, and he continued to wear his gun until he got to Socorro.

The two Texas law officers made another demand which likewise met with no cooperation from Henry. He was asked to ride in the front seat of the car with Dwight, while the law officers rode behind, to see that he did not try to escape en route. "And have one of you sons of bitches drill me from behind?" he said. "Hell no! I'm getting in the back seat."

It might be imagined that these two Texas men were quite nervous about their mission, that Dwight Craig might have given them a good warning about the speed and accuracy of Henry's shooting. Anyway, they seemed satisfied to compromise on several points. Henry went with them of his own volition, because he most certainly could have killed them both before they could have drawn their guns, had he decided upon that course of action. Perhaps the reason he decided otherwise was out of deference to his friend Dwight.

Henry had stolen so many cattle it just wasn't safe for him around Quemado. He was gone in Old Mexico for several months at the time he jumped his bond. But he sneaked back to see his wife, who was living there at the Goat Ranch.

One of the J. boys happened to ride up on him one day when he was driving a bunch of cattle. Henry threatened him, saying, "If you ever tell you saw me, I'll kill you." And then he rode on, because he figured that fellow wouldn't talk. But J. did. He went for help.

Several of us was working for Tom Curtis, putting up hay. We were getting $1.50 a day. One of the men helping with the haying was Jim Cheatham. He had never had any trouble with Henry, but he had been through World War I, and he had the name of being a dead shot with a rifle.

Well, one day while we were on that haying job, Tom rode down where we was working, and he called Jim over to where he was and they had a long talk. After they got through talking, Jim went and got his horse and rode off with Tom, and we didn't see either one of them again for several days.

When Henry's activities got so bad that no one's stock was safe from his pilfering, he was finally killed by a sheriff's posse, near the Goat Ranch.

When Henry Coleman was killed, he was wrangling horses early one morning. He was shot by a posse of five men, who might have been there all night, waiting for him. His wife could see what was happening from the house, and Henry— she could see he was hit—rode out of sight behind a little ridge and down into an arroyo. She wanted to go to him but they wouldn't let her. They didn't go over there themselves either, because they thought he might still be alive. He bled to death in this draw, but no one knew it until evening, because only then would anyone venture over there, and then they found out that he had been dead for quite a few hours. Ray Morley and another man went out there the next day and his body had still not been moved.

There were two shots fired at Henry that hit him, and I think he must have laid out there most of the day after he was first shot. He was shot in the groin. Dr. Thomas in Magdalena examined him later, and he said that that first shot severed an artery and even knocked his hip bone out of its socket; he would have bled to death in a short time.[1]

When they found him, he was backed up against a little cedar tree and he and his six-shooter cocked and in his hand. Some said that right after they shot him the first time, a couple of men in the posse put their hats on sticks and pitched them up over the top of that little ridge, and Henry drilled holes in those

hats right quick, so they knew better than to show themselves
and go to where he was.

*State of New Mexico vs. T. M. Curtis, James Albert
Cheatham, John Cox, M. M. Coleman and Ralph Windsor,*
January 9, 1924[2]

At the October Term of Court, 1923

That T. M. Curtis, James A. Cheatham, John Cox, M. M. Coleman
and Ralph Windsor were held to await the action of the Grand
Jury on the charge of unlawfully killing one Henry Coleman, alias
Street Hudspeth, which said killing was charged to have occurred
in Catron County on the 15th day of October, A. D. 1921.

NO TRUE BILL

Not indicted for murder

Magdalena News—October 22, 1921,
HENRY COLEMAN KILLED

Henry Coleman, as he was known to residents of this county,
was shot to death by members of a sheriff's posse near what is

known as the Goat Ranch, about thirty miles from Quemado last Saturday morning. A warrant for the arrest of Coleman issued out of a justice court in Catron County, was placed in the hands of T. M. Curtis, upon learning that Coleman was in the county, organized a posse composed of John T. Cox, J. A. Cheatham, Ralph Windsor, M. M. Coleman and himself, and proceeded to Coleman's ranch to make the arrest. It is reported that just about sunup, Coleman came on horseback towards the posse, and that immediately upon the attempt to make the arrest, the gunfight ensued which resulted in the death of Henry Coleman. A coroner's jury was empaneled, and rendered a verdict that Henry Coleman came to his death from gunshot wounds at the hands of officers of the law, while they were attempting to arrest him.

District Attorney Fred Nicholas went to Quemado and made an investigation of the killing. He reports that the members of the sheriff's posse appeared before Dionicio Lopez, justice of the peace, and waived preliminary hearing and were held to await the action of the grand jury upon their own recognizance.[3]

Mr. Nicholas states that he has found nothing in his investigation so far as to indicate that the affair was anything but a justifiable killing.

The body, which was brought to Magdalena, showed that [there were] two bullet wounds, one on the right side of the neck, ranging downward into the body and the other on the left leg.

Some of the best information on Coleman's death comes from "Salty John" Cox:

One member of our posse had had law training, and he had recently been elected a J. P. It was through his efforts that the five-man posse was able to organize and go after Henry legally. I wasn't proud of my part in it—to have to kill a man—but something had to be done. This stealing was going on, on a big scale and you couldn't catch Henry or bring him to justice. He had been caught red-handed; they got him indicted with more indictments than you could shake a stick at, and still he got out of it. He jumped his bond and went to Mexico. And he went right on stealing.

One family lived pretty close to Henry's place at Goat Springs, and they tried to keep track of him. Through careful and patient watching, they found out that Henry was back in the country, after a several months' stay in Mexico. He had slipped back to see his wife, and he was getting ready to pull out for good. He knew he'd used up all his time around here—he couldn't stay here no longer and be healthy. Well, what he was doing—he was trying to gather up all his cattle and trying to take them clear out of the country. I think he was aiming to go down into Mexico with them. Mrs. Coleman and her brother were out there with him, at the Goat Ranch.

We'd been watching him, and we found out that the first thing he did of a morning was to wrangle his horses. Them horses had to go east or north from the corral, and we knew he would usually ride out that way. There was a little hill northeast of the house just a little way, and he used to ride up on that and look all around.[4]

When we found out that he was in there, gatherin' up them cattle an' fixin' to pull out for good, we had to work fast. We got our warrant put in order, and we gathered up our bunch to go after him. We had to work real quiet—never told nobody what we aimed to do. We rode over that way one day, and dropped into a little sheltered place quite a way from his house, and we laid out there all night. The next morning, we took our places right over the ridge from where he lived.

Just at daybreak, we rode up towards the little hill that was his lookout. We knowed he'd head for that the first thing. We met him just as we was coming over that hill. He was coming towards us, about two hundred yards away. We yelled "Halt!" to him, but he broke into a run, then, headin' east. The shooting started. Henry was armed, but he wasn't trying to shoot. He was aiming just to get away. One shot—no one knew whose shot it was—went through his leg above the knee. He was ridin' a little sorrel horse, and the horse started to buck. Yes, I know they said the horse bucked him off but that wasn't so. He wasn't bucked off, but I could see he was trying to get away from that horse— trying to step off. He did get away from him, finally, and he got down into a little draw. There were trees and bushes in that draw and Henry could work his way up or down the draw and we couldn't see him. He was behind a little ridge.

We started to work them ditches. We was careful not to get too close. Had to be he could have shot us from cover. Finally, Jim Cheatham he worked around to where he could see Henry, down behind a bush in this draw. Jim was a good shot and had a cool nerve to go with it. He located Henry, and with his rifle, he sent a second shot that hit Henry in the back of the neck. He quivered a little; that was all. He maybe was already dead, or almost dead. I'd say that second shot was fired about eight o'clock in the morning, or a little later, and about an hour or so after the first shot.

Henry's wife and her brother come out then and got him, an' took him down to the house. His wife was tellin' how nice he looked, after she got him laid out down there. He was a good lookin' feller, you know.

I never thought that any of them men figured on taking Henry alive. He's slipped through their fingers time and again. They got it all fixed up legal when they went after him, but they didn't figure on giving him any break—couldn't afford to.

They'd laid out all night, and of course they was awful nervous, especially one of 'em that hated Henry the most. They'd gone out there to kill him, and they was ready to go to desperate ends to do it. There was a lot of timber just west of that little bare hill. The trees was thick along this little pass, an' I think that's where they really was. They could get a good shot from them trees, without bein's seen. They couldn't hardly risk meetin' Henry out in the open like they said they did. He'd have got at least one of them, maybe more. So you couldn't blame 'em.

As soon as we got in shootin' range, they all turned loose at once. Cheatham was a real shot with a rifle. He might have been the one that got him through the leg. We know he was the one that got him with that last shot, but chances are, he was already dead by then.[5]

But anyway, I believe that they didn't none of them ever figure on bringin' Henry in alive.

The newspaper account of the death of Henry Coleman was
gleaned from the *Magdalena News*, and had been run again, verbatim,
in the *Socorro Chieftain*.

What I was particularly struck by in this article was the rather
prosaic attitude taken towards this very dramatic event. There
were no sensational headlines used; simply the statement "Henry
Coleman Killed." The facts were not played up at all. It would
seem that the subscribers were just not too much interested in such
rural rough stuff!

Outlaws hardly even rated front page coverage in those days.
The front page of the *Chieftain* was for the most part taken up with
the activities of a local politician. The written lines trotted along after
him in the manner of an obsequious manservant, noting every move
he made and how he looked and what he wore.

Other main topics were the social gymnastics of Mesdames
Jones and Smith, who vied with each other in pouring tea or coffee
at fashionable town get-togethers. What they described in detail
included the expression "with accessories of such-and-such a color,"
had not yet been dreamed up by the society editors. There were all
the elites, and the trying-to-make-the-grade elites, and the ones
who knew they didn't rate as leaders of fashion, but they could give
parties anyway, and get their names in the paper once in a while!
The ladies of Socorro were really in there, according to the *Chieftain,* scrambling for status just as little towns everywhere always
have and these affairs were going on at a great rate, so that Henry
Coleman, riding his horses in the hills one hundred miles or more
to the west, and living the life of one of the last authentic outlaws,
was little more than a myth, and not one that aroused much interest
locally. His death, and the events leading up to it, simply did not
make much of a dent in the porcelain-armored surface of the society
folk of the little town. It is doubtful whether they had any idea of
the realness of the drama involved, or that it was the pure essence of
the stuff that the miraculous TV of the future would someday spew

forth. The life of the range beyond the hills that climbed out of the Rio Grande Valley was another world.

There was nothing more about the case in subsequent issues—no sustained interest whatsoever.

I found one more personal account having to do with Henry's death, which was told me by Charlie, the old man who had once been Henry's chore boy at the Goat Ranch.

I knew Jim Cheatham pretty well, and after I went to work over in Arizona, I saw Jim over there, and he told me quite a bit about the killin'. He was in that posse, y' know. He said that when Henry got down into the arroyo, they couldn't see him no more, an' they didn't dare show themselves. They didn't know how bad he might be hurt, or if he was alive. They wasn't takin' no chances.

They stationed one or two men where they could see him if he tried to go out of there, to the east or southeast. Finally, after they waited around there nearly all day, someone ventured to where they could see him. He had braced himself against a cedar tree, an' he had his six-shooter aimed against the skyline. An' Henry was dead.

Notes

1. Born at Garnettsville, Kentucky, on November 7, 1878, Dr. Robert A. Thomas attended the National Normal University at Lebanon, Ohio, and graduated from Louisville Medical College in Louisville in 1904. Upon graduation he married Cora Belle Burkbridge and opened a practice at Bowling Green, Kentucky, before he moved to Magdalena in 1907. He may well have been the most beloved physician in Socorro County history. He had an office not only in Magdalena but also in Kelly, where he served the miners there. Said to have been an "earnest Democrat," he opened the Magdalena Pharmacy in 1914 and aided the community and a large part of Catron County until his tragic death on April 25, 1937. Thomas was driving three miles west of Magdalena when he fell asleep and crashed into a deep arroyo and

died instantly. *Santa Fe New Mexican*, January 22, 1912; *Albuquerque Journal*, April 25, 1937; 14th Census (1910), 15th Census (1920), 16th Census (1930), Socorro County, NM; Ralph Emerson Twitchell, *Leading Facts of New Mexico History*, 5 vols. (Cedar Rapids, IA: Torch Press, 1912), 4:369.

2. In the 1920 census, Ralph Windsor and his wife, Juanita, were living near Salt Lake along with their 1-year-old son, Jesse. Windsor listed his occupation as a cowboy and said he owned his own ranch. Windsor was born in Hood, Texas, on January 31, 1896. His World War I draft card has him as tall, with light hair and blue eyes. The son of David and Addie Windsor, he was raised on a farm at Hale Center near the village of Plainview in Hale County, Texas. For a time his younger brothers Erastus and Detch also ranched near Salt Lake. In 1930 Windsor was working on a ranch he purchased near Holbrook, Arizona, where a second son was born. Windsor died on March 13, 1964, at Stamford in Jones County, Texas. 13th Census (1900), Hale County, TX; 15th Census (1920), Socorro County, NM; 16th Census (1930), Navajo County, AZ; Texas Death Certificates, 1903–1982, Ancestry.com, accessed July 6, 2021.

    Thomas Merrill Curtis was born on September 27, 1876, in Bosque County, Texas. Curtis attended school through the sixth grade and, on June 19, 1899, at 23, married Rosa Profitt and moved in with his in-laws in Young County, Texas. Two boys were born of the marriage. Rosa died at age 27 in 1907, leaving Curtis to raise the boys by himself. Curtis later married Kitty Viola Simpson, seventeen years younger, and the couple moved to Monument in Lea County, New Mexico. Six children were born of the second marriage. Tom and Kitty Curtis moved to the Quemado area during World War I and filed on land west of Quemado. Tom and his older son, Bill, drove the family cattle and horses west from Monument while Kitty and the younger children traveled by train to Magdalena and then by Model T to the homestead. Curtis was tall, of medium build, with blue eyes and light-colored hair. After serving as deputy sheriff in the 1920s, the hardworking cattleman acted as brand inspector and game warden in the 1930s. He died in the hospital in Socorro at the age of 89 on February 23, 1966, and was buried in the Quemado Community Cemetery. Kitty died in 1972 and was put to rest beside her husband. McKee-Roberts, *Dust to Dust*, 180; *Albuquerque Journal*, February 24, 1966; World War I Draft Registration Card, Ancestry.com, accessed July 6, 2021; 11th Census (1880) and 13th Census (1900), Young County, TX; 15th Census (1920), Socorro County, NM; 16th Census (1930) and 17th Census (1940), Catron County, NM.

Although ranching near Quemado, Marion Mobley "Max" Coleman was not related to Henry Coleman. M. M. Coleman was born at Granbury, Texas, on January 11, 1889. Of medium build and medium height, with gray eyes and light brown hair, he listed his occupation on his World War I draft registration card as "farmer and ranchman." Coleman claimed he was the first person from the South Plains to graduate from the Agricultural and Mechanical College of Texas, or what became Texas A&M University, saying he financed his education by catching wild horses. Married to Jennie Mae Cannon in September of 1913, Coleman and his wife were frequent visitors to Magdalena. At one time Max was a Socorro County deputy sheriff and a friend of Henry Coleman. Max related stories and legends of the fabled Lost Adams Diggings, which he spent five years unsuccessfully searching for before finally concluding that he had spent more money searching for the elusive Adams Diggings than it was worth. Max would later write, however, that the horse Henry Coleman was riding at the time he was killed had been stolen from his ranch. M. M. Coleman was enumerated on the 1920 census at Quemado by Adolfo L. Chavez as "Colmen." He was later active in promoting the Ocean-to-Ocean Highway and was selected secretary of a committee in Quemado to promote tourism. Coleman claimed that at one time he controlled 50,000 acres of ranchland and had a herd of 1,200 cattle and 500 horses. Leaving New Mexico, he returned to the family home in Lubbock, Texas, where he became a prominent attorney and wrote several articles for *Frontier Times*. After suffering a stroke late in life, Coleman wrote a set of memoirs of life in the Southwest that was published in 1953 as *From Mustanger to Lawyer*. Surprisingly, he had nothing to say about Henry Coleman. After spending his last few years in a nursing home, Coleman died of a cerebral hemorrhage at West Texas Hospital in Lubbock on December 4, 1968. He was 79. 12th (1900), 13th (1910), and 15th (1930) Census, Lubbock County, TX; 14th (1920) Census, Socorro County, NM; World War I and World War II Draft Registration Cards, Ancestry. com, accessed July 10, 2021; Max M. Coleman, *From Mustanger to Lawyer* (San Antonio: Carleton, 1953), part A and part B; Max Coleman, "The Adams Diggings," *Frontier Times* 12, no. 4 (January 1935): 137–38; Santa Fe *El Nuevo Mexicano*, May 13, 1920; *Albuquerque*

Morning Journal, May 10, 1920, and March 5, 1922; *Lubbock Morning Avalanche*, February 24, 1953; *Lubbock Avalanche Journal*, March 26, 1968. His obituary appears in the *Lubbock Avalanche Journal* on December 5, 1968.

Cheatham is most likely James Albert Cheatham, who was born in Brown County, Texas, on June 29, 1887, and who was a wagoner in the Veterinary Corps during World War I. He appears on the 1900 census in Brown County, the son of Nancy Josephine Short and James Albert Cheatham Sr. The same James Cheatham appears on the 1910 census in El Paso County as a "cowboy" and a "wage earner." His World War I draft registration card in June 1917 has him "horse raising" with a broken hand and working for the Culberson County Road Department at Kent. Although Cheatham cannot be located in the 1920 census, he appears in the 1930 census, now 43, as a "farm laborer" in Deaf Smith County on a "stock farm." His World War II draft registration card in April 1942 has him weighing 176 pounds, five-feet, six-inches in height, and with gray hair. At age 52 he is back in Brown County with no income and living with his mother. Cheatham had a second-grade education. According to Langford Johnston in his *Old Magdalena Cow Town*, Coleman had such a disliking of Cheatham that he swore he would kill him on sight. Cheatham died of broncho-pneumonia in the Veterans' Hospital at Temple, Texas, on January 20, 1965, at the age of 77 and was buried in the Clear Creek Cemetery at Bangs, nine miles west of Brownwood in Brown County, Texas. "James Albert Cheatham," *Find a Grave*, accessed May 1, 2021, https//www.findagrave.com/memorial/7376019/james-albert-cheatham; 13th Census (1900), Brown County, TX; 14th Census (1910), El Paso County, TX; 16th Census (1930), Deaf Smith County, TX; 17th Census (1940), Brown County, TX; Johnston, *Old Magdalena Cow Town*, 24–25; World War I and World War II draft registrations cards, Ancestry.com, accessed July 5, 2021, https://www.ancestry.com/genealogy/records/james-albert-cheatham-24-7yk0wq.

3. The elderly Dionicio Lopez owned a sheep ranch along Rito Quemado Creek a few miles east of the small community. He appears on the 1930 census as living alone at age 76; 16th Census (1930), Catron County, NM.

Fred Nicholas was born in Las Vegas, New Mexico, on July 25, 1883. His family moved to Colorado, where Nicholas attended the University of Colorado. He graduated from the University of Michigan

Law School in 1907 and moved to Magdalena in 1918. Two years later he was appointed the district attorney for the Seventh Judicial District of Socorro, Valencia, and Sierra Counties. He was elected four consecutive times and later moved to Albuquerque, where he continued to practice law and was influential in Republican politics until he became ill in 1941. Nicholas died of a stroke in Pueblo, Colorado, on April 10, 1946. World War I Draft Registration Card, Ancestry.com, accessed July 20, 2021; 13th Census (1900), Denver County, CO; 15th (1920) and 16th Census (1930), Socorro County, NM; 17th Census (1940), Bernalillo County, NM.

4. The sandrock-topped hill that rises a few hundred feet above the countryside where Henry Coleman rode every morning and where he died is actually northwest of the Goat Ranch.

5. "Salty John" Cox later bragged that he was the man who fired the fatal bullet. Ironically, Cox and Coleman were the best of friends for many years in southern New Mexico and rustled cattle together after Coleman's escape from the Juárez jail. In the Quemado area, however, for reasons Cox never explained, they became bitter enemies. Bryan, *True Tales of the American Southwest*, 93–107.

Epilogue

N ot much is left to tell. What remains is in the nature of what you would call "mop-up operations." One little angle concerns the whereabouts of Henry's old standby, Ben Foster. It is natural to suppose that when Henry sneaked back into the country and tried to gather his cattle together and make a clean getaway, he would have needed some good help, and what better or more reliable source could he have tapped than the services of his faithful Ben?

Most popular accounts have it that on that fateful morning when Henry rode to his death, Ben was there with him at Goat Springs, and that when the shooting started, Ben made his way from either the house or the corral and took refuge inside of the spring—the tunnel of water in the hill above the house. If he did it must have been a pretty chilly deal; and since we have variations in the accounts of how much time elapsed after the first shot was fired until they shot again and either finished Henry off or found that he was dead, it is possible that the accounts that tell that Ben soaked in that spring water the entire day might be correct.

This story ties into another account, which would depict Ben Foster's next jump, in an attempt to keep a little ahead of fate or justice or both! As soon as the posse had departed from the vicinity of Goat Springs, Ben pulled his saturated self together and emerged from his cold storage haven, saddled a horse, and rode as fast as he could to the home of a Spanish American neighbor who lived on the west side of the Largo Creek. His friend was not at home, and Foster just went into the house, horse and all. Most of the adobe homes of the Hispanos still had dirt floors, but Foster was not worrying about any floor. He would have taken his horse in with him even if the place had had marble tiles!

He stayed in there all night, and along toward morning he changed horses, "borrowing" a little gray horse from his host's and leaving his own mount, which was probably ridden down anyway. From there he hopped from one hideout to another, eventually making his way into Old Mexico, where he boasted to a friend that he would be back and kill every son of a bitch who was in that posse.

Another version differs radically from this by saying that Ben Foster was not at the Goat Ranch when Henry Coleman was killed there, but was down in the Horse Mountains, between Datil and Horse Springs, and that when the word reached him about Henry's death, he went down into Old Mexico and was never seen or heard of in these parts again. The stories that claim that he was at Goat Springs outnumber the few that claim otherwise. Certainly, if he had been there, he would not have been advertising the fact.

Still another version of Ben, bent upon hectic flight, comes to us. A friend of Henry's who lived down near Horse Springs said that Ben Foster came by his place riding a black, bald-faced horse on his way to Mexico. His host on this occasion suspected that Ben wanted to change horses, but he didn't ask for one; he merely asked for the way to the ranch of one Perry Grogan, who was down toward Beaverhead. Directions were given: how to go by way of Coyote Peak and thus save seven or eight miles. Ben rode on his way never to be seen again in the community of Quemado.[1]

One more account about Ben adds a timely flourish to his desperate story. There was a man living in Catron County, which was separated from Socorro County only a matter of months before Henry's death. His brother went to Mexico, married a native Mexican woman, and spent the rest of his life south of the border. He knew Ben Foster and had this to say during a brief reunion with his brothers: "I seen a feller hangin' to a tree down in Old Mexico, and I'm right certain it was Ben Foster."

And so both the legend and the facts lose the momentum that made them spin along so fast for a while. Far faster than ten ordinary men's lives all rolled into one! The intricate machinery that reflected Henry Coleman's character, his force and daring, his expert conniving, his tireless comings and goings—all the complex things that formed the man and his motives—became merely a dead carcass devoid of his wild spirit gone to God knows where. In terms of machinery, the delicately balanced mechanism of such extraordinary power became sadly and finally inanimate—an object capable only of collecting rust. And no longer, in some homes where a penchant for mystery and excitement took precedence over the dullness of actual facts, could some mothers roll their eyes dramatically and say to naughty little children, "You better be good, or Henry Coleman will get you!"

Good friends who knew that Henry had his share of a sense of fair play, of generosity, more than his share of courage and bravado, and a love of life and of certain people who did not fit the prescribed pattern and yet were genuine in their own way—many missed him and grieved his passing.

An aftermath of the Old West with much of its mercurial glow existed in Henry. Those who viewed his life, firsthand, saw something akin to the late, late movies on television—a return of an old plot, surprisingly well done.

All of Henry's traveling was done on horseback; the good and noble horses that he rode were a part of his life and the manner of men who lived between 1850 and 1900. He made many, many tracks in his life, and they were nearly all horse tracks.

His family in Texas seemed—or perhaps they chose—to recede into the background. In modern times it might be said that they became neutralists, noninterventionists. They had come to his aid at different times in his life, but toward the end of his life, they were not much in evidence. Perhaps they took a dim view of the declining respectability involved in aligning themselves with Henry's latest escapades.

Funeral services for Henry were held in the K. P. Hall in the old cow town of Magdalena, farthest outpost of a branch line of the Santa Fe Railroad. One of the few people who was present at these services was Marvin Ake, who now ranches southeast of Datil. He was 7 or 8 years old in 1921.[2]

It was my first funeral, and I'll never forget it. I can see it now, just like it was yesterday. Evidently Henry was a friend of my

family's. They all went to the funeral and took me along—guess
because they didn't have nobody to leave me with! I was all
slicked up and in my best clothes, and I was scared to death.

But I was curious too. I wanted to go, scared as I was. I'd
never seen a dead person before, and of course I wanted to see
him. The hall was a big, long, bare place. There used to be lots
of things going on in it in them days—not only an occasional
funeral, but meetings of all kinds, and elections, and lots of
dances.

There was only a handful of people there—perhaps twenty or
so. They didn't near fill up that hall, so they was all up at one end
of it, near the door. There was little folding chairs put there for
people to sit on.

Henry's casket was off to one side. I don't remember there
being any flowers at all. The widow sat right by the casket, and
she cried and sobbed real hard all through the whole thing. I
don't believe there was even a minister there, but often times
there wasn't at those country funerals. Often, just some friend
would get up and tell something about the dead person, about
when they were born, and all that; and maybe someone would
recite a prayer, and that would be it.

One of my clearest memories of the whole thing was how a
Magdalena woman got up and sang a song. In them days women
hadn't taken to wearing much make-up yet, and that was the first
woman I'd ever seen all painted up, with powder and rouge like
an actress. It made a big impression on me. She got up and sang
in a very loud, trembly voice. Her voice rang extra loud in that
bare hall. There wasn't even any piano to play along with her.

Then the people filed by the casket, to take a last look at
Henry. That's the part I'd been waiting for, scared as I was. But I
had to go up and look at him. He was all dressed up in a dark suit
and a white shirt, with a necktie on. I remember how white that
shirt was. His hands were folded over his chest, and there was
a big diamond ring on one of his fingers. I wondered if it was
real; in fact, after the funeral, I heard several people remarking
about it. I wondered if they took it off before they buried him.
My father might have been one of the pallbearers. I can't remember whether he was or not.

Henry, like the wife who preceded him in death, lies in an unmarked grave in the Magdalena cemetery. Authorities who took his body into Magdalena wired his relatives in Texas some message to the effect of "What shall we do with him?" It was thought that the family would probably want his body to be sent on to Texas. The answer came back tersely: "Bury him."[3]

Notes

1. Fifty-three-year-old Perry Grogan, who lived near Beaverhead, is listed on the 1920 Census as a small farmer; 15th Census (1920), Socorro County, NM.

    Coyote Peak, 8,364 feet high, is some twenty miles south of Horse Springs, three miles off the southwestern edge of the San Agustin Plains.

2. Marvin Parvis Ake was born in Socorro on March 11, 1913, and died at his ranch near Datil, on March 10, 1994. A little over a year after Ake married Bessie A. Bannerman on April 17, 1934, his 35-year-old father, Robert Valentine "Vol" Ake, was shot and killed in front of the Beaverhead Post Office on August 6, 1935, by 53-year-old Aaron Lucien Inman, a neighbor and rancher. In what newspapers called the Catron County Feud, the two neighboring ranchers had been quarreling for several months over a property boundary. Ake had allegedly ridden to Inman's ranch near Indian Peak three weeks earlier, waving a rope in the air, threatening to rope Inman. "The next time I see you, I am going to have my .30 and you had better have yours," Inman remembered Ake saying. Spotting Ake at the Beaverhead Post Office three weeks later, Inman opened fire with his rifle, shooting Ake once through the body and once in the head. Inman was charged with murder and brought to trial in Reserve in November 1935. It was the most sensational trial in Catron County history, with the largest crowd Reserve had ever seen—hundreds of friends of Ake and Inman, many unable to find accommodations were camping out, and crowded into the village. At the trial every inch of standing room was filled as citizens listened at doorways and windows. "High crowned hats and high heeled boots" were everywhere, the *Albuquerque Journal* noted. After a week-long trial and nineteen hours of deliberation, the jury found Inman guilty of

involuntary manslaughter, and the judge sentenced him to ten years in the state penitentiary. Inman immediately appealed the decision to the state supreme court. Three years later, in the summer of 1938, Inman was in Las Cruces meeting with his attorney on his appeal when he happened to meet two of Ake's sons, 20-year-old Robert, a freshman at New Mexico A&M College, and 23-year-old Roscoe, who was at a CCC camp in the Mesilla Valley. In a shootout Inman critically wounded Robert in the chest and shot Roscoe in the right arm. Robert was rushed off to a hospital in El Paso, Texas, where after weeks of critical care he recovered. Both sides were charged in the case, and after a series of trials, transfers of venue, and newspaper headlines, neither Inman nor the young Ake brothers were convicted. Shortly thereafter Inman's case before the supreme court was denied, and he was ordered to serve his ten-year sentence. Shortly before he was to enter the state penitentiary in Santa Fe, Governor Clyde Tingley issued him a pardon. By this time Inman had moved to Buckhorn in Grant County. He died at Truth or Consequences at the age of 72 in 1958. He was buried in Magdalena, not far from where Robert Ake had been laid to rest twenty-three years earlier. Ironically, Robert "Vol" Ake and Aaron Inman, bitter enemies, were both born in Pontotoc, Mason County, Texas. Somehow, after Henry Coleman's death, Marvin Ake gained possession of his Colt revolver, which the Ake family retains to this day. 15th Census (1920), Socorro County, NM; 17th Census (1940), Catron County, NM; 17th Census (1940), Grant County, NM; *Albuquerque Journal*, August 9, October 25, November 10 and 24, 1935, May 9 and July 30, 1936, and July 23, 1938; *Clovis* (NM) *Evening News Journal*, August 7, 1935, and May 9, 1936; Marvin Ake family tree, Ancestry.com, https://www.ancestry. com/family- tree/person/tree/14767802/person/18010295980/facts?_ phsrc=Cmq109&_phstart=succe; Aaron Inman family tree, Ancestry. com, https://www.ancestry.com/search/?name=aaron_inman&event=_ catron-new+mexico-usa_533&name_x=_1 (both family trees accessed July 13, 2021).

3. Claude Hudspeth, who had been elected to Congress from West Texas in 1918, was in Washington, DC, when he received the news that his brother was dead. "It was a great shock to me, and a cloud of depression has hung over me since I got the wire last Sunday night," Hudspeth told George W. Wallace, his law partner in El Paso. Only recently, when Coleman had jumped bail, had he visited with his brother in El Paso. "I did everything within my power to avert

it and prevent him from going back, and that was that he would be ambushed and given no chance," the congressman wrote. Hudspeth had wired his brother Roy at Sonora, Texas, to "go to Magdalena at once." The next day he sent a telegram to Jerry Wheeler, a friend in Magdalena who ran a drugstore and who knew Henry well. Hudspeth urged Wheeler to have Henry "put away properly." Wheeler went to the Goat Ranch to "examine the scene" and "found things as the posse reported." Members of the posse, Wheeler went on to say, were some of Coleman's "bitterest enemies," especially John Cox, who had tried to assassinate Coleman only days before Henry fled to El Paso. "Henry had no chance whatsoever," Wheeler continued. The druggist had met Roy Hudspeth in Socorro and the two had driven to Magdalena to make funeral arrangements. After the funeral and his return to Texas, Roy Hudspeth stopped in El Paso, where he was met at the train station by George Wallace. Wallace relayed the news to Claude Hudspeth in Washington that Henry had been buried in Magdalena, where "a large number of his friends were present and expressed great sorrow over the unfortunate affair." The posse learned that Henry was back at the Goat Ranch, Wallace said, and that it was his custom to ride out to a small knoll about a half mile from the ranch shortly after dawn to look for his saddle horse. C. B. Hudspeth to Jerry Wheeler, October 17, 1921 (telegram); Hudspeth to Wheeler, October 18, 1921 (telegram); Geo. [Wallace] to C. B. Hudspeth, October 21, 1921; Claude B. Hudspeth to George W. Wallace, October 25, 1921, all in Hudspeth Papers. "Cattle Rustler's Magdalena Grave Gets New Headstone," Socorro *El Defensor Chieftain*, October 8, 2020.

Life of Eleanor Williams

Helen Cress

Life in a remote area with little law enforcement, even today, enabled entrepreneurial characters like Henry Coleman to prosper and gave my mother, Eleanor Williams, a history to pursue for posterity. She wrote under the pen name Mel Jewell because many people who had known Coleman were still living in the area at the time she was recording her story.

Eleanor became interested in Henry Coleman, I believe, because she had an insatiable curiosity, a vivid imagination, and an interest in preserving accurate history to the extent possible for future readers. Learning the real story behind a man so debonair, polite, and of apparent impeccable manners—who was also well-dressed, handsome, and yet so daring and so skilled with his wit and his gun— had to have had tremendous appeal for her. Such seemingly opposing forces in a single personality would have definitely intrigued her, because she was an extroverted person herself, with tremendous interest in what made others "tick," what forces forged their outlook on life. Coleman seemed to epitomize both the good and the bad in an especially alluring manner.

Another factor that had to have lured her to his story would have been that she was an eastern-bred woman who was never attuned to or felt any affinity with the area or the lifestyle she was born into, and as a young girl in her teens, she had come west on the train from Pittsburgh, Pennsylvania, to visit close family friends who ranched in Montana. There she fell head over heels in love with the West and all things western. She remained enamored until her death.

I feel certain that, once she heard a few tales of Henry Coleman's exploits and the reactions of some of his victims, she would have become fascinated by him. She would have been intrigued by the duplicity of his personality, his ability to exhibit many positive and admirable characteristics and, at the same time, dark and depredating behaviors that allowed him to steal from true friends as readily and easily as from strangers, to abuse the rights and livelihoods of those who had gone to great lengths to accommodate him, and to jump bail and disappear, probably into Mexico, when he knew friends who were not well-to-do by any stretch had paid his bail and then were just without the money they had spent and would not get it back.

But first and foremost, Eleanor was an artist, and this trait drove her personality to a large extent, beyond her drawing and painting to a talent for writing; she produced poetry, short stories, and historical biographies. I believe her artistic leaning was the primary progenitor of her decision to write Henry Coleman's story. And once she had the idea, it took on a mind of its own and had to be carried to fruition.

Eleanor was born Eleanor Lockwood McClintock, the first child of Norman and Ethel McClintock. The McClintocks were an old and prosperous Pittsburgh family who owned a Persian rug business there and were among the socially elite of that city. This is one of the things about her that I find most admirable—that, although she was cultured and well-educated, none of these supposed benefits seemed to matter to her, and when she left the area, it was with a rodeo hand who was definitely not prosperous, and she lived with him in a small picket two-room house south of Quemado, New Mexico, when they began housekeeping. Prior to that she camped outdoors with the rodeo crowd they traveled with, or stayed in inexpensive hotels that were probably not cockroach-proof!

Her father and her uncle Walter were apparently wanting to escape the rug business, because Norman took up photography as a young man. He developed the time-lapse concept, but unfortunately, he did not patent it and someone else did. He worked throughout the United States as a wildlife photographer and lectured at Rutgers University on his photography. Uncle Walter was part of a group sent out by Grover Cleveland (undoubtedly during his second presidency) to look at prospective land for designation as national forest. The group took along a Blackfeet Indian guide to lead them, and Uncle Walter developed a lasting kinship with the tribe and tried for most of the remainder of his life to represent them and their concerns to government officials; he was even adopted into the tribe and took Mad Wolf as his adoptive father. He wrote two books about the Blackfeet—*The Old North Trail* and *Old Indian Trails*—and published many photographs of their tepees and way of life. My aunt told me that my grandfather Norman was probably the one who did much of the photography. They would have had to take along the cumbersome glass plates and other developing paraphernalia and pack these things on mules.

Eleanor, I believe, had some of Uncle Walter's genetic makeup in terms of her spirit of adventure, and this also would have contributed to her fascination with Henry Coleman's story. She was bright and excelled at every task she attempted. She was well-educated, and I believe largely self-educated, because, as far as I know, she only went through high school at Westover School in Middlebury, Connecticut—a highly rated college-preparatory school and finishing school—and possibly one semester at Penn State. I had often read the term "finishing school" but had to look it up to see what it actually meant. The definition I discovered said "school for young women that focuses on teaching social graces and upper-class cultural rites as preparation for entry into society." I then thought, "No wonder she scorned the East and took up with western ways!" But after all this, she studied art at, I believe, Carnegie Tech in Pittsburgh and later at Art Students League in New York City with a renowned artist, and that was probably for at least two years. And she obviously did well in this pursuit.

Eleanor seems to have had an innate knowledge of to whom she should go in order to get things done, as exemplified on several occasions. She had shocked her straight-laced family, I am sure, by eloping with a rodeo hand, Walter Heacock, and notifying her parents only after they were married. Walter immediately signed the couple up to go to South America with a Wild West show he had signed on with, and he and some of his rodeo acquaintances had been hired to perform down there. While there she began to learn some of the elementary rudiments of trick riding. The troupe went to Chile, and after several performances, the employers, who had not yet paid a dime to the performers, left town in secrecy, leaving the riders there with no money and no means to return to their country of origin! Eleanor was the one who struck out to find the American consulate in Santiago to ask for assistance in returning home. They were told the married couples would be sent back to the United States first, and then the rest would go. So Eleanor and Walter were taken to a hotel from which they were to return by boat to their own country the following day, but Walter got an attack of acute appendicitis in the night and they had to find a surgeon to operate on him that night. Consequently, they were unable to make the trip for two more weeks. When finally able to travel, they were allowed to make the voyage on a Japanese fishing barge, which discharged them on the coast of California.

The newlyweds had several lean years of following the rodeo circuit across the country; then Eleanor was ready to put down roots. They purchased three hundred acres of land south of Quemado, and that was the original parcel of what has grown to be the Williams Ranch. The house on their acreage was a two-room picket house with plaster, but Eleanor was proud of it.

Again, Eleanor was the one who took action when a neighbor, Tom Teefenteller, who lived about two miles south of Eleanor and Walter, argued with them about the location of their property line. His claim, if correct, would have significantly decreased their holdings. He tried to erect a fence where he wanted it, and Eleanor met him in court, having researched for herself the facts and presented her case and all the required legal records; she won the case. She even requested a resurvey of this area, and whether because of her input or not, a resurvey was done in 1933, and the section line markers can be found that depict that. Perhaps this survey was done to employ men during Roosevelt's attempt to provide work for the many who were suffering during the Great Depression. Regardless, it was important, because the previous survey had been done in the 1880s.

Eleanor rode in rodeos with Walter for several years, performing as a trick rider, and even did some bronc riding, but fortunately did not continue that. They covered the entirety of the country, and during her time with the rodeo crowd, she did some wonderful pencil drawings of the rodeo performers they knew, both men and women, to create a priceless collection. She and Walter separated in 1934, and she left with her adored, well-trained, and dependable paint horse Sonny Boy, whom she pulled in a wooden trailer behind her car, and went to her parents in Pittsburgh. She and Walter had a 4-and-a-half-year-old daughter who was with Eleanor's parents in Pittsburgh. Once Eleanor was home, her father helped her obtain a job, and of course jobs at that time were not easy to find. Her position involved working in the kitchen of a mental health facility, then called an asylum. This employment did not coincide with Eleanor's idea of a way to spend a life, so when she came across an advertisement put out by Ringling Brothers and Barnum and Bailey Circus wanting people to perform in the coming season, she eagerly responded and was hired and instructed to travel that fall to Sarasota, Florida, to start her fall training in preparation for the 1935 season. So she once again loaded Sonny Boy into his trailer and pulled him to Sarasota for their new life, again leaving little Nan with her parents. Her circus performances involved trick riding and an aerial act. In the spring the circus went on tour around the country and she stayed on until they closed down in the fall and returned to Sarasota.

In the divorce settlement with Walter, Eleanor had had to divide the property in New Mexico with him, but ultimately she stayed on and he left. She had returned after leaving Ringling Brothers and had to determine how she was going to complete the house Walter and his brothers had been building, which had walls and flooring but needed much more construction. She remarried, and this marriage produced a second daughter. Eleanor had sent for her daughter in Pittsburgh, and her mother returned with Nan. Eleanor had the new baby and a 7-year-old, and the house to be completed. She had some paying guests at the ranch in the summers, so earned some money that way. And some local men with construction experience completed the building project. Her second marriage was never a success, apparently, and did not last. In 1940 she married Frank Williams, whom she always considered the love of her life. They built the ranch up to the size it came to be by buying up every small operator who was selling their land until they had the land they managed until Frank died in 1974. Three more children resulted from this marriage.

Throughout the 1950s and early 1960s, Eleanor painted many fine oil paintings, real character studies of some of the area's most interesting representatives of the local culture. Commissioning a painting for someone who wanted an elegant-appearing beauty put on display for general admiration did not interest her. She wanted to depict strong character and ordinary, hard-working subjects. An amazing talent she displayed was the ability to get an excellent, accurate likeness of her subject, but she was also able to capture the essence of their personality. Her collection of portraits, painted in oils over the 1950s and 1960s, comprise a wonderful and varied portrayal of life in the Southwest.

One feature of Eleanor's story about Henry Coleman that I found admirable was her ability to present what she learned in her interviews and to allow her readers to make their own interpretations of what she wrote. Having arrived in New Mexico and bought property ten years after Henry's death, and often obtaining conflicting renditions of a story from several folks she questioned, she might have put forth strong opinions of her own, but she left it to the reader to choose what possibilities existed as truth. Also, her research was extensive and thorough; she pursued it over many months, maybe as long as one to three years. She and Frank traveled numerous miles as they learned of new sources of information, both interviewing and taking photographs to be used with the story. They visited the Goat Ranch and photographed the house Henry had lived in with Minnie, his second wife—or, more accurately, the wife that followed Clara, because his marital history before he arrived in New Mexico is unknown. One person who accompanied them and in fact took them to the Goat Ranch was Juan Cordoza, who furnished reams of helpful information, having worked for Henry at some time. Juan seems to have experienced the more positive aspect of Henry's disposition and likely did not own livestock for Henry to prey upon. Sometime during her friendship with Juan, Eleanor painted a portrait of him.

In fact Henry had befriended many of the Spanish American inhabitants of the area, but that did not mean that they were exempt from losing livestock to him if they owned livestock that he found handy.

Eleanor's life ended in June of 1979 at the age of 72 after a brief illness. She had never recovered from the loss of Frank four years and some months earlier, and she seemed to lack the will to continue without him. She developed pneumonia, which she did not attempt to treat. It seemed as if she were just preparing for the end.

By the time her son discovered that she was extremely ill and called an ambulance to transport her to the hospital, her lungs were full, and she never responded to treatment. She lived only about a week. She had been able to see her story on Henry Coleman published in eight installments of a little magazine at that time put out by Socorro Electric Cooperative, but she never attempted to do more with it. Here readers can enjoy her exceptionally well-researched and well-written account in full.

Bibliography

Books

Adams, David Wallace. *Three Roads to Magdalena: Coming of Age in a Southwest Borderlands, 1890–1990*. Lawrence: University Press of Kansas, 2016.

Alexander, Bob. *Lawmen, Outlaws and S.O.Bs*. Vol. 2, *Gunfighters of the Old Southwest*. Silver City, NM: High Lonesome Books, 2007.

Ball, Larry D. *Elfego Baca in Life and Legend*. El Paso: Texas Western Press, 1992.

Barrett, S. M., ed. *Geronimo: A True Story of America's Most Ferocious Warrior*. New York: Skyhorse, 2011.

Bryan, Howard. *Incredible Elfego Baca: Good Man, Bad Man of the Old West*. Santa Fe: Clear Light, 1993.

Bryan, Howard. *True Tales of the American Southwest: Pioneer Recollections of Frontier Adventures*. Santa Fe: Clear Light, 1998.

Bullis, Don. *Unsolved: New Mexico's American Valley Ranch Murders and other Mysteries*. Los Ranchos, NM: Rio Grande Books, 2013.

Burton, Jeffrey. *The Deadliest Outlaws: The Ketchum Gang and the Wild Bunch*. Denton: University of North Texas Press, 2009.

Caffey, David L. *Chasing the Santa Fe Ring: Power and Privilege in Territorial New Mexico*. Albuquerque: University of New Mexico Press, 2014.

Camp, Ben, and Dykes, J. C. *Cow Dust and Saddle Leather*. Norman: University of Oklahoma Press, 1968.

Coleman, Max M. *From Mustanger to Lawyer*. 2 vols. San Antonio: Carleton, 1953.

Crichton, Kyle S. *Law and Order, Ltd.: The Rousing Life of Elfego Baca of New Mexico*. Santa Fe: Rio Grande Press, 1970.

Curry, George. *George Curry, 1861–1947: An Autobiography.* Edited by H. B. Hening. Albuquerque: University of New Mexico Press, 1986.

de la Garza, Phyllis. *The Apache Kid.* Tucson: Westerlore Press, 1995.

Erwin, Allen A. *The Southwest of John Horton Slaughter: Cattleman -Sheriff.* Spokane: Arthur H. Clark, 1997.

Fence Lake, New Mexico Area: Families & History. Fence Lake, NM: Fence Lake Book Committee, 1985.

French, William. *Some Recollections of a Western Ranchman, New Mexico, 1883–1899.* New York: Frederick A. Stokes, 1928.

Hayes, Jess G. *Apache Vengeance: The True Story of the Apache Kid.* Albuquerque: University of New Mexico Press, 1954.

Herman, Daniel Justin. *Hell on the Range: A Story of Honor, Conscience, and the American West.* New Haven, CT: Yale University Press, 2010.

Hillerman, Tony. *The Great Taos Bank Robbery and Other Indian Country Affairs.* Albuquerque: University of New Mexico Press, 1973.

Hinton, Harwood P. *History of the Cattlemen of Texas: A Brief Resume of the Live Stock Industry of the Southwest and a Biographical Sketch of Many of the Important Characters Whose Lives are Interwoven Therein.* DeGolyer Library Cowboy and Ranch Life Series 1. Reprint, Austin: Texas State Historical Association, 1991.

Hogan, Patrick. *Prehistoric Settlement Patterns in West-Central New Mexico: The Fence Lake Coal Lease Surveys.* Albuquerque: University of New Mexico Office of Contract Archeology, 1985.

Hutton, Paul Andrew. *The Apache Wars: The Apache Kid, the Hunt for Geronimo, and the Captive Boy Who Started the Longest War in American History.* New York: Crown, 2016.

Johnson, Maureen G. *Placer Gold Deposits of New Mexico.* Washington, DC: United States Government Printing Office, 1972.

Johnston, Langford Ryan. *Old Magdalena Cow Town.* Albuquerque: Cottonwood Printing, 1983.

Julyan, Robert. *The Place Names of New Mexico.* Albuquerque: University of New Mexico Press, 1996.

Klump, Kathy Bliss. *The Last Roundup of the "Y" Cattle Company.* Wilcox, AZ: PetKat Publishing, 2016.

Kohout, Martin Donell. "Joseph Henry Nations." *Handbook of Texas Online.* Accessed September 7, 2021. http://www.tshaonnline. rog/about/people/martin-kohout.

McKee-Roberts, Kathryn. *From Dust to Dust: Cemeteries in Northern Catron County.* Bosque Farms, NM: self-published, 2006.

Metz, Leon Claire. *The Shooters: A Gallery of Notorious Gunmen from the American West.* New York: Berkley Books, 1996.

Miller, Darlis A. *Open Range: The Life of Agnes Morley Cleveland.* Norman: University of Oklahoma Press, 2010.

Niederman, Sharon. *A Quilt of Words: Women's Diaries, Letters & Original Accounts of Life in the Southwest, 1860–1960.* Boulder, CO: Johnson Books, 1988.

Owen, Valerie. *Byrd Cochrain of Dead Man's Corner.* Snyder, TX: Feather Press, 1972.

Paddock, B. B. *History and Biographical Record of North and Western Texas.* Vol. 2. Chicago: Lewis Publishing, 1906.

Pagan, Edwardo O. *Valley of the Guns: The Pleasant Valley War and the Trauma of Violence.* Norman: University of Oklahoma Press, 2018.

Sager, Stan. *Viva Elfego! The Case for Elfego Baca, Hispanic Hero.* Santa Fe: Sunstone Press, 2000.

Thompson, Jerry. *A Civil War History of the New Mexico Volunteers and Militia.* Albuquerque: University of New Mexico Press, 2015.

Thrapp, Dan L. *Victorio and the Mimbres Apaches.* Norman: University of Oklahoma Press, 1974.

Twitchell, Ralph Emerson. *Leading Facts of New Mexico History.* 5 vols. Cedar Rapids, IA: Torch Press, 1912.

Wagner, Jim. *Datil: A Hidden History of an Historic New Mexico Town.* Self-published, 2022.

Westphall, Victor. *The Public Domain in New Mexico, 1854–1891.* Albuquerque: University of New Mexico Press, 1965.

Westphall, Victor. *Thomas Benton Catron and His Era*. Tucson: University of Arizona Press, 1973.

Articles

Bell, Bob Boze. "The Blast at Steins Pass." *True West Magazine*, July 15, 2014.

Caudill, Oscar. "Hell on the Largo." *Frontier Times* 46, no. 1 (January 1972):6–9.

Coleman, Max. "The Adams Diggings." *Frontier Times* 12, no. 4 (January 1935): 137–38.

Cress, Helen. "Murders Most Foul." *Catron County Historical Society Newsletter* (January–February 2014).

Jewell, Mel [Williams, Eleanor]. "Outlaw Born too Late." *New Mexico Electric News* 14 (7, 8, 9, 10, 11); 15 (1, 2, 3) (August 1964–March 1965).

Kayser, David. "Fort Tularosa: 1872–1874." *El Palacio* 79, no. 2 (September 1973): 24–29.

Kayser, David. "The Southern Apache Agency." *El Palacio* 79, no. 2 (September 1973): 16–23.

Kohout, Martin Donell. "Claude Benton Hudspeth (1877–1941)." *Handbook of Texas Online*. Accessed May 27, 2021. https://www.tshaonline.org/handbook/entries/hudspeth-claude-benton.

Secrest, Clark. "'Black Jack Died Game': The Bandit Career of Thomas E. Ketchum." *Colorado Heritage Magazine* 30, no. 4 (2000).

Thompson, Jerry. "Gunfight at the NH Corral." *Wild West* 10 (April 1998): 42–47, 78.

Thorp, N. Howard. "Henry Coleman." *Southwest Crossroads*. Accessed June 1, 2021. https://www.southwestcrossroads.org/search.php?query=N.%20Howard%20Thorp.

Upchurch, Alice Gray. "Apex, TX." *Handbook of Texas Online*. Accessed June 1, 2021. https://www.tshaonline.org/handbook/entries/apex-tx.

Westphall, Victor. "The American Valley Murders." *Ayer Hoy en Taos: Yesterday and Today in Taos County and Northern New Mexico* (Fall 1989), 3–9.

Census Data

Apache County, AZ, 1900.
Bandera County, TX, 1880.
Beckham County, OK, 1910.
Bernalillo County, NM, 1900, 1910, 1920, 1930, 1940.
Bosque County, TX, 1870, 1880.
Brooks County, GA, 1870.
Brown County, TX, 1900, 1940.
Catron County, NM, 1930, 1940.
Coconino County, AZ, 1940.
Colfax County, NM, 1880.
Cooke County, TX, 1880.
Crockett County, TX, 1900.
Curry County, NM, 1910.
Deaf Smith County, TX, 1930.
Denver County, CO, 1900.
Doña Ana County, NM, 1900, 1910, 1920.
Drew County, AR, 1870.
Eddy County, NM, 1910, 1930.
El Paso County, TX, 1910, 1920, 1930, 1940.
Garza County, TX, 1920.
Grant County, NM, 1930, 1940.
Hale County, TX, 1900.
Johnson County, TX, 1900.
Lea County, NM, 1930.
Los Angeles, CA, 1930.
Lubbock County, TX, 1900, 1910, 1930.
Luna County, NM, 1900.

Mahnomen County, MN, 1920.
Marion County, AR, 1870.
Mason County, TX, 1880.
McKinley County, NM, 1920, 1930, 1940.
Multnomah County, OR, 1940.
Navajo County, AZ, 1930.
Ochiltree County, TX, 1900.
Palo Pinto County, TX, 1880, 1900, 1910, 1920.
Pottawatomie County, OK, 1910.
Red River County, TX, 1860.
Ringgold County, IA, 1910.
Roger Mills County, OK, 1900.
San Saba County, TX, 1880.
Santa Fe County, NM, 1870.
Scurry County, TX, 1900.
Sierra County, NM, 1885, 1900, 1910, 1940.
Socorro County, NM, 1870, 1880, 1900, 1910, 1920, 1930, 1940.
Sterling County, TX, 1910.
Trinity County, TX, 1870.
US Indian Census, 1891, 1892, 1895, 1900, 1930.
Valencia County, NM, 1870, 1880, 1920, 1930.
Young County, TX, 1880, 1900.

Archival Collections

Eleanor Williams Papers. In possession of Helen Cress.
Claude Benton Hudspeth Papers. Special Collections, University of
    Texas at El Paso Library.
Jerry Thompson Collection.
Post Office Appointments. Ancestry.com.
Quemado Justice of the Peace Records. Catron County Clerk's Office,
    Reserve, NM.
Socorro County Clerk's Records. Socorro, NM.

World War I Draft Registration Cards (M1509). Record Group 163, National Archives and Records Administration, Washington, DC. All available on Ancestry.com.

World War II Draft Registration Cards (M1962). Record Group 147, National Archives and Records Administration, Washington, DC. All on Ancestry.com.

Newspapers

Abilene Reporter (TX)
Albuquerque Democrat
Albuquerque Journal
Albuquerque Morning Journal
Albuquerque Tribune
Arizona Republic (Phoenix)
Belen News (NM)
Catron County News (Quemado, NM)
Christian Worker
Clovis (NM) *Evening News Journal*
Corpus Christi Caller
Deming (NM) *Graphic*
Deming (NM) *Headlight*
Eagle (Silver City, NM)
El Defensor Chieftain (Socorro, NM)
El Hispano-Americano (Belen, NM)
El Nuevo Mexicano (Santa Fe, NM)
El Paso Herald
Estancia News Herald (NM)
Farmington Times Hustler (NM)
Fort Worth Star-Telegram
Gallup (NM) *Independent*
Las Vegas (NM) *Daily Gazette*
Las Vegas (NM) *Gazette*

Lincoln County Leader (Toledo, OR)
Lubbock Avalanche Journal
Lubbock Morning Avalanche
Reserve Advocate
San Angelo (TX) *Standard*
San Saba (TX) *News*
Santa Fe Gazette
Santa Fe New Mexican
Sierra County Advocate (Hillsboro, NM)
Star & Times (St. Louis)
Tampa Bay Times
Weekly Phoenix Herald
West Schuylkill Press and Pine Grove Herald (Tremont, PA)
Victoria (TX) *Advocate*

Index

A

Acoma, NM, 6
Agua Chiquita Creek, NM, 65
Ake, Marvin Parvis, 163
Ake, Robert Valentine "Vol," 163
Ake, Roscoe, 164
Alamogordo, NM, 103
Albuquerque Journal, 7, 17, 19, 66, 99,
　102–4, 114, 131–32, 141–42, 154,
　163–64
Alcatraz, CA, 38
Alderete, Francisca, 140
Aldridge, Mattie, 76
Ambrosio Lake, NM, 132
American Valley Sheep and Cattle
　Company, 8
Anderson, Charles, 38
Anderson, Mary Ann, 73
Andrews, Hank, 12
Anson, TX, 12, 18, 54
Apache (Ndé), 6–7, 9–12, 17, 19,
　35–36, 38, 105
Apache Creek, NM, 9, 12, 19
Apache Kid (Hasjat-bay-nag-ntay), 35, 38
Apache Kid Peak, NM, 38
Apache Kid Wilderness, NM, 38
Apache Mountain, NM, 10
Apex, TX, 42–43
Aragon, NM, 12
Arizona Territorial Prison, Yuma, AZ, 38
Armijo, Fidel, 14–15
Armijo, Geronimo, 12
Armstrong, George, 110–11, 113
Armstrong, Nettie Shepard, 113
Atkins, Dave, 36
Atkinson, Henry, 8
Auguste, Frederic, 11

B

Baca, Adelaida, 101
Baca, Anastacio, 130
Baca, Antonio J., 110
Baca, D. B., 2
Baca, E. B., 117
Baca, E. C., 110, 133
Baca, Elfego, 2, 12–15, 95, 107–8,
　110, 141
Baca, Eliseo, 140
Baca, Enriqueta, 131
Baca, Epifanio, 89, 92, 101, 111
Baca, Flora, 108
Baca, Joseph Simon, 131
Baca, J. S., 124, 141
Baca, María Ignacia, 108
Baca, Nazario Garcia, 136–37, 140
Baca, N. G., 13, 110
Baca, Pedro, 101
Baca, Steve, 111
Ball, Eva, 108
Bandera, TX, 29
Bandera County, TX, 29
Bangs, TX, 156
Barnwell, SC, 99
Bastrop, TX, 76
Beaverhead, NM, 160, 163
Beckham County, OK, 101, 107
Beeville, TX, 75
Belen, NM, 7, 103, 107–8, 113, 130,
　132, 140
Bell County, TX, 101
Bell Ranch, TX, 37
Belton, TX, 101
Billy the Kid, 1, 51
Blake, G. W., 123
Blake, Zora A., 100
Bosque County, TX, 65, 154
Bosque Redondo, NM, 7
Bosson, William Herbert, 54
Bourbonnaise, Aaron F., 73–74
Bourbonnaise, Antoine (Anthony) A. S.,
　73–74
Bourbonnaise, Arthur Levi, 74

Bourbonnaise, Aurelia. *See* Thompson,
    Aurelia Bourbonnaise
Bourbonnaise, Frank, 67, 74, 90,
    96–98, 114
Bourbonnaise, Isabelle, 137
Bourbonnaise, Lola, 137
Bourbonnaise, Mary Ozetta, 74
Bourbonnaise family, 88, 120
Bourguet, Nellie, 140
Bowling Green, KY, 153
Brawner, Catherine Frances "Kate," 106
Brewster County, TX, 131
Bronco, TX, 100
Brown County, TX, 156
Buckhorn, NM, 83, 164
Burbage, Ollie Mae, 114
Burkbridge, Cora Belle, 153
Burnett's Texas Sharpshooters, 42
Bustamante, Clara, 140
Bylesby, Harry M, 75
Bylesby, Ozette, 75

C

Camp Fremont, CA, 83
Cañada Alamosa, NM, 7, 141
Cannon, Jennie Mae, 155
Canyon de Chelly, AZ, 7
Capes, John J., 74
Carranza, Venustiano, 131
Carrejo, Ambrosio, 14–15
Carrejo, Enrique, 14
Carrejo, Juan, 14–15
Carrejo, Nellie Whiskers, 14
Carrizozo, NM, 99, 105
Carter, Lige, 66
Casey, James, 10–11
Casey, John P., 9
Catron County, 1, 3, 5, 23–24, 27,
    66–67, 99–101, 104, 107, 120–21,
    131–32, 148–49, 153, 155–56,
    163–64
Catron, Thomas Benton, 8–9, 15, 19
Cattlemen's Protective Association, 8
Caudill, Faro Wilson, 106
Caudill, Frederic "Fred," 95, 100, 106,
    110–13

Caudill, John Asbury, Sr., 106
Caudill, Oscar Debs, 95, 100, 106,
    110–13, 137
Caudill, Oscar York, 105
Caudill, Rosie, 106
Chavez, Adolfo L., 155
Chavez, Candelario, 14
Chavez, Maria Ursula, 141
Cheatham, James Albert, 156
Cheatham, James Albert, Sr., 147–48,
    151, 153, 156
Chickasaw Nation, OK, 74
Childers, James Benjamin, 101
Childers, Miram, 101
Chloride, AZ, 38
Chloride, NM, 105
Choat, Sophia Ellender, 42
Church of Jesus Christ of Latter-Day
    Saints (Mormons), 3, 9, 64, 132
Cibola National Forest, 38
Cimarron, NM, 104, 120
Ciudad Juárez, Chihuahua, Mex., 3–4,
    34, 65–66, 157
Clarendon, TX, 74
Clarksville, TX, 103
Clayton, NM, 37, 114
Clearwater, FL, 75
Cleveland, Agnes Morley, 120–21
Clifton, AZ, 60, 83
Cobb, Zach Lamar, 29
Cochrain, Byrd, 14–15, 19
Cold Creek, TX, 42
Cole County, MO, 99
Coleman, Clara, 4–5, 39, 42–43, 52,
    69–73, 75–76, 78, 86–92, 95–97,
    100–101, 110, 112, 115–21, 123–24
    death, 92, 95, 115, 117–19
    home, 88–89, 96, 117, 119, 123
Coleman, Henry, 1–5, 14, 16, 24–29,
    31–43, 45–55, 57–64, 66, 69–73,
    77–82, 85–86, 92–98, 115–20,
    123–32, 135–39, 143–53, 155,
    159–65, 167–69, 172–73
    death, 97, 152–53, 160, 172
Coleman, Lee, 36
Coleman, Marion Mobley "Max," 155

Coleman, Minnie, 128, 133
Coleman-Oliver murder case, 109–10, 112
Collins, Lola B., 76
Collins, Othello, "Ody" D., 75
Columbia University, NY, 120
Concho, AZ, 104–5
Cooney, NM, 12
Cooper, Bruce, 14–15
Cooper, Clay C., 14
Cooper, Harmon, 14–15
Courtright, James, 10–11
Cow Springs Ranch, NM, 65–66
Cox, John Thomas "Salty John," 2–3, 38, 60–61, 65–66, 148–49, 157, 165
Cox, John William, 65
Cox, Robert, 65
Cox, Slash J. L., 61
Coyote Peak, NM, 160, 163
Coyotero Apaches, 7
Craig, Agnes Helen, 140
Craig, Dwight Andrew, Jr., 140
Craig, Dwight Andrew, Sr., 136, 140, 144–46
Craig, Elizabeth, 140
Craig, Georgia, 140
Craig, Maud Chrisolm, 140
Craig, Sally, 139
Craig, Samuel Milton, 139
Crapper, Caliste A., 74
Cress, Helen, 16, 54, 167
Crockett County, TX, 29
Cullen, Ed, 33, 36–37
Curtis, Thomas Merrill, 137, 147–49, 154

D

Dalton, Roy, 111–12
Datil, NM, 76
Datil Mountains, NM, 8, 75
Davis, Jarrette, 12, 18–19
Davis, John, 12, 19
Davis, Minnie C. See Coleman, Minnie
Deaf Smith County, TX, 156
De Baca County, NM, 140
Deming, NM, 17, 141
Deming Headlight, 17, 38, 141
Dillingham, Cora Elizabeth, 100

Dowell, Jim, 3
Drag-A Ranch, NM, 120
Drew County, AR, 29

E

Eaton, William Ethan, 114
Eaton, William J., 112, 114
Eaton de Chavez, Marie Marcillene, 114
Eaves, Coke Hamilton "Hamp," 132
Eaves, Marie Kaiser, 132
Ellston, IA, 100
El Malpais, NM, 6
El Paso, TX, 54–55, 100, 102, 105, 107–8, 156, 164–65
El Paso County, 55, 105, 156
Elsinger, Robert, 10–11
Engle, Edna Eugenia, 100
Engle, Edwin Edgar, 100
Engle, Frederick Melvin, 100
Engle, Katherine Adela, 100
Engle, Lola Mae, 100
Errick, J. P., 110
Escondido Mountain, NM, 6, 88, 101
Estancia, NM, 101, 103
Estes, Albert, 83
Estes, Emily, 83
Estes, Richard, 83
Estes, Robert E. Lee, 83
Estes, Sealy, 83
Estes, Seely Cosby, 83

F

Farmington, NM, 132
Farr, Dave, 99
Farr, Ed, 99
Farr, George Adam, 99–100
Farr, George David, 99
Farris, Sophia, 116
Field Creek, TX, 42
First National Bank of Magdalena, 121
Flagstaff, AZ, 105
Florida Mountains, NM, 4
Folsom, NM, 37
Fort Craig, NM, 6
Fort Tularosa, NM, 7
Fort Union, NM, 104

Fort Wingate, NM, 6
Fort Worth, TX, 11, 106
Foster, Ben, 50, 54, 80–82, 90, 95, 110,
    118–19, 127, 137–39, 159–60
Fox Mountain, NM, 81–82

G

Galisteo, NM, 114
Gallo Basin, 9
Gallo Canyon, NM, 10
Gallo Mountains, NM, 6–11
Gallo Springs, NM, 9–12
Gallup, NM, 49, 81, 132, 139–40
Garnettsville, KY, 153
Garza County, TX, 100
G-Bar Ranch, AZ, 34, 38
Geronimo (Goyaalé), 6, 12, 38, 141
Gila River, NM, 6
Gila Wilderness, NM, 5
Goat Ranch, 1–2, 16, 123–24, 128–30,
    133, 143–57, 160, 165, 172–73
Gonzales County, TX, 54
Gonzales, Ramon, 11
Graham, Fannie, 76
Graham, James A., 76
Granbury, TX, 155
Grant County, NM, 83, 164
Grants, NM, 132
Grayson, TX, 103
Griffith, S. C., 110
Grogan, Perry, 160, 163
Grossetete, Adella, 12
Grossetete, Alexis, 10, 18
Grossetete, Clotilde, 10–11, 18
Gruglia, Lucy W., 102
Guadalupe County, NM, 113
Gulf, Colorado and Santa Fe Railroad, 43
Guyon, Geraldine Lola, 74
Guyon, Joseph Francis, 74
Guyon, Joseph Napoleon, 74

H

Hale Center, TX, 154
Hale County, TX, 154
Hall, Alice May, 104
Hall, Hezekiah, 93, 104, 111

Hall, Nathan, 104
Hall, Nathan, Jr., 104
Hannett, A. T., 102
Harmony, NM, 100
Hazard, KY, 106
Heacock, Eleanor. *See* Williams, Eleanor
Heacock, Walter, 169–71
Henderson, George W., 54, 104–5,
    137–39
Henderson, Lucy, 105
Henderson, Mary, 105
Henderson, Sarah Elizabeth
    "Lizzie," 103
Hicks, Ida Mae, 54
Higgins, Patrick, 11
Hillsboro, NM, 4, 17, 35, 40–42, 65,
    103, 141
Hokit, Green K., 42
Holbrook, AZ, 154
Hood, TX, 154
Horse Camp, NM, 55
Horse Springs, NM, 12, 99, 111,
    160, 163
Hot Springs (Truth or Consequences),
    NM, 106
Hubbell Cattle and Sheep Company, 37
Hubbell, Frank, 37, 55
Hubbell's Draw, NM, 55
Hudspeth, Claude, 3, 16, 25, 28–29, 36,
    124, 128, 131, 164–65
Hudspeth, Claude Benton, 29, 131
Hudspeth County, Texas, 25
Hudspeth, Elizabeth Ann, 131
Hudspeth, Henry Street. *See* Coleman,
    Henry
Hudspeth, Henry Street, Jr., 28
Hudspeth, Landrus, 28
Hudspeth, Mary Elizabeth, 29
Hudspeth, Roy, 3, 165
Hunt, Alice Casey, 86, 99
Hunt, Charles Lucas, 99
Hutchinson, Ben, 43
Hutchinson, Walter J., 39, 43

I

Inman, Aaron Lucien, 163–64

J

Jackson County, KS, 74
Jackson County, MO, 113
Jenkins, Cliff, 34, 38, 40, 59
Jewell, Mel. *See* Williams, Eleanor
Jewett Gap, NM, 9, 14
J. H. Nations Meat and Supply
    Company, 55
Johnson, Langford, 17, 75
Jones County, TX, 154

K

Keith, Albert, 4
Kendall, William C. "Billy," 65
Kent, TX, 156
Ketchum, Thomas Edward "Black
    Jack," 37
King, Israel, 3
Klepper, Johnie May, 132
Klepper, Lorenzo M., 132
Klepper, Rebecca Eliza "Obie," 132

L

Lake Valley, NM, 66
Largo Creek, 3, 7–9, 39, 70, 75, 86–87,
    101, 105–6, 159
Las Cruces, NM, 4, 66, 99, 164
Las Vegas, NV, 17, 101, 156
Latham, Sarah Dean, 65
Lavaca County, TX, 54
Lea County, NM, 100, 103
Lebanon, OH, 153
Lemitar, NM, 140
Leopold, Aldo, 101
Leopold, Estella, 101
Lincoln County, NM, 1, 99
Lohn, TX, 42–43, 116
Lone, NM, 99
Long Beach, CA, 105
Lopez, Dionicio, 149, 156
Lopez, Francisco, 108
Lopez, Severo (Sebero), 96, 108, 110, 124
Loraine, TX, 106
Lordsburg, NM, 36–37
Los Angeles, CA, 141
Lovington, NM, 103, 132

Lubbock, TX, 155–56
Lujan, Eugene, 103
Luna County, NM, 17, 29, 43
Luna County Democratic Party, 4
Luna, Solomon, 102
Lynch, Claude, 104
Lynch, Jesse, 104
Lynch, John C., 103–4
Lynch, Joseph, 104
Lynch, Maria, 103
Lynch, Thomas, 103

M

MacGillivray, Katherine, 103
Madrid, José Maria, 6–7
Magdalena, NM, 28
Magdalena Stock Driveway, 99
Mahnomen County, MN, 75
Mangas, NM, 17, 57, 66, 101, 130, 140
Mangas Coloradas, 6
Mangas Mountains, NM, 6–7, 65
Mangas Valley, NM, 7–8
Manzano Mountains, NM, 99
Marion, AR, 28
Mason County, TX, 66
Maxwell Land Grant, 8, 102
Mayfield, W. B., 110
McAdams, Caroline G. "Callie," 106
McAllister, Daniel H., 9, 11
McCabe, Lola, 75
McCarthy, Charlie, 12, 107
McClellan County, TX, 75
McClintock, Eleanor Lockwood.
    See Williams, Eleanor
McClintock, Walter, 168
McCulloch County, TX, 42, 116
McCustion, Cox, 65
McCustion, Noah, 65
McIntyre, James, 10–11, 18
McKinley County, NM, 54, 140
McPherson, Ada, 120
Mechem, Edwin L., 113
Mechem, Merritt Cramer, 113
Medina County, NM, 131
Medina River, TX, 28–29, 131
Mesilla Valley, NM, 164

Middlebury, CT, 169
Middle Frisco, NM, 12–13, 107
Midland, TX, 54
Miles, John, 132
Miller, Harris, 121, 130, 144
Milligan, Grant, 15, 66
Milligan's Plaza, NM. *See* Upper
    Frisco, NM
Mimbres, 5
Mimbres Apaches, 17, 144
Mimbres peoples, 5
Mineral Wells, TX, 76
Mitchel, Charles, 110
Mitchell County, TX, 106
Model, Faro, 110
Model, Jose, 110
Model, Marie, 111
Mogollon, NM, 12
Mogollon peoples, 5
Monticello, AR, 28
Moore, W. C., 10–11
Morley, Agnes. *See* Cleveland,
    Agnes Morley
Morley, Lorraine, 120
Morley, Ray, 65, 115, 120, 147
Morley, William Raymond, Jr., 120–21
Morley, William Raymond, Sr., 120
Mormons. *See* Church of Jesus Christ of
    Latter-Day Saints
Mosheim, TX, 65
Moulton, TX, 54

N

Nations Draw, NM. *See* Hubbell's
    Draw, NM
Nations, Eli, 54
Nations, Joseph Henry, 54, 56
Nations Land and Cattle Company, 55
Navajo (Diné), 6–7, 154
Negrito Creek, 11
Neighbor, Hugh, 67, 96, 98, 108
Neighbors, H. M, 110
New Deal, 16
New Mexico Cattle Growers
    Association, 43, 120
New Mexico Livestock Board, 43

New Mexico Sanitary Board, 42–43
New Mexico School of Mines (New
    Mexico Institute of Mining and
    Technology), 104
New Mexico Sheep Sanitary Board, 43
New Mexico State Corporation
    Commission, 131
New Mexico State Penitentiary
    Board, 141
New Mexico State Police, 132
New Mexico Territorial Council, 113
NH Ranch, NM, 14, 18
Nicholas, Fred, 54, 149, 156–57
Noe, George Kristead, 124, 130
Norman, Eugenia Mae, 17–18, 38, 100,
    121, 168–69
Northern New Mexico Stock Growers
    Association. *See* New Mexico
    Livestock Board

O

Ochiltree County, TX, 75
Ojo Caliente, NM, 7
O'Keeffe, Georgia, 29
Oliver, Cap Hill, 76
Oliver, Donovan Mackey (Don), 71–72,
    76, 89–93, 95–97, 100, 110–11,
    115, 119
Oliver, Edward Dionysius, Jr., 67, 76,
    95–96, 98, 105, 110, 118
Oliver, Edward Dionysius, Sr., 76, 105
Oliver, Roy Scott, 76
Omaha, NE, 130
Otero, Manuel Antonio, 101
Otero, Manuel B., 93–94, 101–2
Owen, Harry P., 19, 93, 95, 102–3, 139
Ozona, TX, 29, 131

P

Padilla, Ana Maria, 67
Padilla, Damian, Sr., 140
Padilla, Felipe, 63, 66, 96–98, 110
Padilla, Francisco, 66
Padilla, José Antonio, 7
Palo Alto, CA, 83
Palo Pinto, TX, 76, 105–7

Palo Pinto County, TX, 76, 105, 107
Pan Flats, TX, 27
Pasadena, CA, 121
Pattes, J. R., 110
Pecos County, TX, 54–55
Pennington, TX, 83
Peralta, Juan, 11
Perry County, KY, 106
Pigeon Grove, WI, 107
Pino, Manuel A., 113
Piño, Selveria, 101
Plainview, TX, 154
Post, TX, 36, 100, 140
Pottawatomie, 73–74
Pottawatomie County, OK, 74–75
Pottawatomie Reserve, OK, 74
Potter, Clarintha. *See* Coleman, Clara
Potter, Theresia, 42–43
Potter, Warren, 42
Prairie View, NM, 67

Q

Quay County, NM, 102
Queen's Head, NM, 14
Queen's Head Mountain, 18
Quemado, NM, 1–2, 16–17, 25, 27–29,
    38–39, 42–43, 46–47, 52–53, 55,
    65–67, 70–71, 73–76, 81, 90–93,
    100–101, 104–5, 111, 128–30,
    132–33, 154–55
Quemado country, 40, 47, 49, 69–70,
    95, 129
Quemado Lake, 101

R

Raton, NM, 102
Raton Pass, NM, 120
Record place, the, 39, 70, 129
Republican National Committee, 102
Reserve, NM, 3, 14–15, 104, 107, 163
Riley, NM, 140
Ringgold County, IA, 100
Ringling Brothers Barnum and Bailey
    Circus, 3, 171
Rito Quemado, NM, 6–8, 17
Rito Quemado Creek, 156

Roger Mills County, OK, 107
Romero, Manuel, 10, 18
Roosevelt, Franklin D., 16, 104, 141, 170
Rosedale, NM, 99
Rural Electrification Authority (REA), 16

S

Sac and Fox Agency, 74
Sacramento Mountains, NM, 34
San Agustin Plains, NM, 15, 60, 99, 163
San Angelo, TX, 17
San Antonio, NM, 114, 141
San Antonio, TX, 28, 131
San Carlos Reservation, AZ, 38
Sanchez, Cruz, 105
Sanchez, Geronimo Eduardo, 141
Sanchez, Josefa, 66
San Francisco River, NM, 7
San Mateo Mountains, NM, 38
San Saba, TX, 37, 43
Santa Fe, NM, 8–9, 66, 102, 114, 130,
    132, 164
Santa Fe Railroad, 43, 120, 161
Santa Fe Ring, 8, 17
Sarasota, FL, 171
Sayre, OK, 100, 106
Schalbar, Elizabeth "Lizzie," 106
Scott, Jake, 104
Scott, Mueller, 10
Sedillo, Antonio Abad, 139, 141–42
Shawneetown, OK, 74
Short, Luke, 11
Sierra County, NM, 66, 103, 107, 141
Silver Lake, KS, 74
Simpson, David, 110
Simpson, Doris, 110
Simpson, Kitty Viola, 154
Simpson, Zelma, 110
Slash JL Ranch, 75
Slaughter, John Bunyan, 12
Slaughter Mesa, NM, 15
Smith, Lydia Augusta, 107
Socorro, NM, 38, 43, 65–67, 75–76, 83,
    100–101, 103–5, 107–8, 131–33,
    140–42, 154–55, 157, 163–64
Socorro Electric Cooperative, 173

Spicer, Marion Clifford, 95, 107
Springerville, AZ, 14, 104–5, 132
Stanford University, CA, 83
Steele, Albert "Abe," 33, 37, 60
Sterling City, TX, 75
St. Johns, AZ, 13, 62–64
Stock Raising Homestead Act
    (1916), 13
Summers, Minnie Lee, 132
Summers, Tom A., 132

T

Tafoya, V. V., 138, 141
Teefenteller, Tom, 170
Temple, TX, 156
Texas Agricultural and Mechanical
    College (Texas A&M University), 155
Thomas, Robert A., 147, 153
Thompson, Aurelia Bourbonnaise, 74
Thompson, Henry J., 74
Thompson, Lola, 74
Thorp, N. Howard, 66
Tingley, Clyde, 164
Topeka, KS, 13, 107
Trinity County, TX, 83
Trujillo Creek, NM, 65
Tularosa River, NM, 9
Tularosa Valley, NM, 7, 15

U

Union, IA, 100
Union County, NM, 37, 99, 114
Upper Frisco, NM, 15

V

Valencia County, NM, 17, 103, 108, 131
Vanderwagen, Edward, 54
V-Cross-T Ranch, NM, 12, 37
Vigil, Gertrude, 137, 141
Villa, Francisco, 32

W

Wade, Edward Clemens Jr., 86, 99
Wallace, George W., 19, 164–65
Ward, John, 3
Warm Springs Apaches, 7
Water Canyon, NM, 104
Waubun, MN, 74
Weatherford, TX, 105
Weed, NM, 65
West Texas State Normal College (West
    Texas A&M University), 29
Wilkes (Wilks), Oran, Sr., 86, 100,
    110–11
Wilkes, Orrin, 110–11
Williams, Eleanor, 3–4, 16, 21, 28, 54,
    106, 167–73
  interest in Coleman, 28
Williams, Frank, 172
Williams Ranch, NM, 170
Wilms, Hazel Clara, 106
Windsor, Addie, 154
Windsor, Jesse, 154
Windsor, Ralph, 148–49, 154
Wolf Wells, NM, 127, 132
Woodbury, TX, 132
Woodruff, Eliza, 54

Y

Y Ranch, NM, 12
Yocum County, TX, 100
Young County, TX, 155
Yuma, AZ, 38

Z

Zamora, Francisco, 136–37, 140
Zuni, NM, 47–49, 51–52, 58, 135,
    139, 144
Zuni Indians, 47, 51, 54, 136
Zuni Plateau, NM, 5
Zuni Salt Lake, NM, 5, 16